Fair Spoken and Persuading

An Interpretation of Second Isaiah

Richard J. Clifford

PAULIST PRESS
New York • Ramsey • Toronto

Acknowledgment

The Publisher gratefully acknowledges the use of excerpts from "Die Dichtungen vom Ebed-Jahwe" in *Das Buch Jesaia* by Bernhard Duhm, published by Vandenhoeck & Ruprecht, Verlagsbuchhandlung, 3400 Göttingen/Postfach 77. Used by permission of the publisher. (Translated into English by the author for inclusion in this text.)

Library of Congress
Catalog Card Number: 83-62016

ISBN: 0-8091-2583-8

Published by Paulist Press
545 Island Road, Ramsey, N.J. 07446

Printed and bound in the
United States of America

CONTENTS

PART TWO
Translation and Commentary of
Isaiah 40–55

ABBREVIATIONS

ANET	*Ancient Near Eastern Texts Relating to the Old Testament* (Ed. James B. Pritchard; 3rd ed.; Princeton: Princeton University, 1969)
BDB	F. Brown, S. R. Driver, and C. A. Briggs, *A Hebrew and English Lexicon of the Old Testament* (Oxford: Clarendon, 1952)
BK	Biblischer Kommentar Altes Testament
BZAW	*Beiheft Zeitschrift für die alttestamentliche Wissenschaft*
CBQ	*The Catholic Biblical Quarterly*
CTA	Andrée Herdner; *Corpus des tablettes en cunéiformes alphabétiques* (Paris: Imprimerie nationale, 1963)
GKC	*Gesenius' Hebrew Grammar as Edited and Enlarged by the Late E. Kautzsch* (2nd English ed. by A. E. Cowley; Oxford: Clarendon, 1910)
HAT	Handbuch zum Alten Testament
HTR	*Harvard Theological Review*
JAOS	*Journal of the American Oriental Society*
JBL	*Journal of Biblical Literature*
JNES	*Journal of Near Eastern Studies*
MT	Massoretic Text
NAB	New American Bible
NJV	New Jewish Version
OG	Old Greek
IQIsa[a,b]	First or second copy of Isaiah from Qumran Cave 1
RSV	Revised Standard Version
TDOT	*Theological Dictionary of the Old Testament* (Ed. G. J. Botterweck and H. Ringgren; Grand Rapids: Eerdmans, 1974f.)
UT	Cyrus H. Gordon, *Ugaritic Textbook* (Rome: Pontifical Biblical Institute, 1965)
VT	*Vetus Testamentum*
*VT*Sup	Supplements to *Vetus Testamentum*

He was a scholar, and a ripe and good one;
Exceeding wise, fair-spoken, and persuading:
Lofty and sour to them that lov'd him not;
But, to those men that sought him, sweet as summer.

King Henry VIII, IV. ii. 50–54

INTRODUCTION

Second Isaiah is the name given by modern scholars to the anonymous author of chapters 40–55 of the Book of Isaiah. The name distinguishes him from "First" Isaiah of the late eighth century to whom the bulk of chapters 1–39 is traditionally attributed, and from the author of chapters 56–66, judged by most scholars to be of the late sixth or early fifth century. Chapters 40–55 are a collection of speeches of the 540's B.C., and perhaps of the following decade, delivered to the Jews who had been deported to Babylon from their native Judah a half century earlier. By the mid-540's, the Neo-Babylonian Empire, which had captured Judah and deported much of its population, was collapsing. The Persian Empire, under Cyrus, was rising to take its place. Such changes in empire caused trepidation and hope in small dependent peoples like the exiled Judahites. Did the shift bode good or ill for them?

Second Isaiah, like his prophetic predecessors, considered the great Eastern empires to be the instruments of his nation's God, Yahweh; the change in empire therefore made a divine statement to Israel. The prophet had to proclaim that statement to his people. The Persian encouragement of deportees to return home and the offer to rebuild native temples signaled for the prophet the end of Yahweh's absence, of his withdrawal "in wrath" because of Israel's sins. He had heard a new and favorable divine decree, "Comfort, comfort my people" (40:1), that set angels and humans upon a new task.

Yahweh's decree directed the exiles to engage in that act through which their ancestors had become Israel in the first place—the Exodus-Conquest, the cosmogonic battle and procession to God's shrine. For Second Isaiah, the Persian policy of allowing the exiles to return to Zion provided the context for the act of obedience that would make the dispirited group Yahweh's people once again. Divine decree in heaven without human response on earth had no

3

meaning for the prophet; he had to persuade his fellow exiles to obey the new word. He therefore arranged the venerable national tradition to speak to the new situation, doing so with wonderful rhetorical skill and sensitivity to the popular temper. The result of his labors is the collection of speeches in chapters 40–55 persuading the Judahites to act according to the decrees of both Yahweh and of his agent Cyrus the Persian: to leave Babylon, to cross the desert, and to assemble in Zion as the restored Israel.

 Second Isaiah is then primarily an orator. His eloquent monotheism, his skill in consoling, the force of his ideas and images, long celebrated by commentators, are all subordinate to his task of persuading. In its insistence that the chapters consist of lengthy and complex speeches, this book differs from most studies of the prophet. That the prophet is "fair-spoken," i.e. eloquent and lyrical, is admitted by all. That he is at the same time "persuading," i.e. practical, given to sustained argument to move people to specific action, is by no means a common interpretation. For most scholars, the chapters are a collection of short pieces, typically from forty-five to seventy discrete units. Many of these, moreover, are thought to be fragmentary or interleaved with later additions. This reading makes of chapters 40–55 an assemblage of pieces too short for genuine development of ideas. The pieces lift the spirit and expand the imagination through images and lyricism, not through argument. The view that Isaiah 40–55 is made up of brief and fragmentrary pieces has the inevitable corollary that the author is a lyric poet rather than a national orator.

The first step then in the study of Second Isaiah the orator must be to demonstrate the original boundaries of his speeches. They must be shown to be of a length sufficient for oratorical argument. The speeches must develop, not merely mention, serious ideas. Our demonstration of length and complexity in the first chapters of the book proceeds negatively and positively. In the second part of Chapter One, the negative demonstration, we note the scholarly distortions that have fragmented the chapters and gutted the speeches of key ideas. We criticize the undiscriminating use in Second Isaiah of two methodologies developed in the analysis of quite different kinds of literature, "literary criticism" (*Literaturkritik,* really discernment of sources) and form criticism. Chapter Two argues positively for the length and complexity of discourse proper to an orator. The chapter illustrates the chief way in which the author develops his thought—through the use of paired ideas or polarities. The pairs are: first and last things, Babylon and Zion, Yahweh and the gods, Israel and the nations, the servant and Israel. Through the interplay of the concepts, some of which appear in every speech, the prophet drives his thought forward. The polarities bear on both style and substance, form and content; thus they are an important clue to the unity of the speeches.

Chapter Three discusses the central idea of Second Isaiah—the new Exodus-Conquest, the new cosmogony. In so doing it makes a case for the large scope and coherence of the speeches. The prophet seeks to persuade the exiles in Babylon that they must now engage in the act whereby a scattered people becomes Israel, the people of Yahweh. They must join in a new Exodus-Conquest, a new cosmogony. Other elements in the prophet's message, first and last things, the nations and their statues, the servant and Israel, draw meaning from the main theme: Israel comes into being in the act of fleeing Babylon and coming to Zion.

The most important part of the book is the translation and commentary of Part II, to which Part I is prefatory. Considerable attention is given in the commentary to defining the boundaries of each speech and to showing its coherence. We propose that there are seventeen speeches. The argument of the speeches is often allusive and elliptical; their rhetoric and logic need elucidation. The commentary attends to the rhetorical development more than to the pre-history of the traditions. Part II demands much of the reader but it is only through the examination of the prophet's own words that we encounter directly his message and test the validity of the proposed thesis.

This book has been kept short in the belief that a small commentary, quickly read, best reveals the coherence and essential simplicity of the oratory. Even if not every detail convinces, I hope that the main thesis will be accepted: *that Second Isaiah in a few closely argued speeches of considerable length urges his fellow Judahites to join him in that act through which they will become Israel.* At any rate, if colleagues are not convinced by the arguments of the book, they will not be wearied by its length.

I have not dealt with some chapters that are arguably Second Isaiah's 34–35 and 60–62, only because I preferred to work within the generally accepted corpus for the demonstration of my thesis. All translations, unless noted, are my own. Chapter and verse citations are according to the *RSV*.

Every preface ought to end with an expression of thanks, for every book is born in a community of ideas and scholars. I have been stimulated by the intuitions and approach suggested by the "Outline of Contents" in James Muilenburg's commentary on Second Isaiah in *The Interpreter's Bible* (Nashville: Abingdon, 1956), V, 415–18. *The New Jewish Version of Isaiah* (Philadelphia: Jewish Publication Society, 1973), done under the editorship of H. L. Ginsberg, has influenced me at every step. A seminar on Second Isaiah under the direction of my teacher, Frank Moore Cross, during my graduate studies has been seminal for me. I have learned much from the approach of Yehoshua Gitay, *Prophecy and Persuasion: A Study of Isaiah 40–48* (Bonn: Linguistica Biblica, 1981). Fr. Robert DiVito and William Propp have read the manuscript and saved me from many errors. Responsibility for all statements, needless to say, is my own.

Much of the book was written during a sabbatical leave spent at the Pontifical Biblical Institute in Jerusalem during the spring of 1982. The leave was supported by the Society of Jesus and by the Weston School of Theology; to both I am extremely grateful. I wish to thank my fellow Jesuits William Dalton, Oscar Rodericks, and Anthony Apukutty for their hospitality and kindness during that time. I am grateful, too, for the use of the Institute library, and for the use of the libraries of Hebrew Union College and the Ecole Biblique.

I dedicate this book to the students of the Weston School of Theology, Cambridge, Massachusetts. Their questions and criticisms, their enthusiasm, and their occasional incredulity have stimulated my interest in Second Isaiah. It is they who have had to listen to many of the ideas in the book. They should be acknowledged publicly as dialogue participants.

PART ONE

The Context and the Message
of Second Isaiah

Chapter One

CONTEXTS ANCIENT AND MODERN

This chapter, prefatory like Chapters Two and Three to the translation and commentary of Part II, sketches the context for understanding Second Isaiah. The ancient context will be described first: Second Isaiah's world and audience (I), then the prophetic tradition within which he spoke (II). The modern context (III) is important too, for it is largely through the categories of the last two centuries of scholarship that we interpret Second Isaiah.

I. SECOND ISAIAH'S WORLD AND AUDIENCE

Redactional introductory verses and biographical narrative that supply information about the other prophets are absent from chapters 40–55; we have only the speeches. The speeches do, however, yield important information about the prophet's world and his audience when they are supplemented by other sources.

The speeches can be dated rather precisely; hence they can be fitted into the events of Babylonian and Judahite history. They must have been written and delivered in the 540's, quite possibly in the 530's as well. They assume that everyone is aware that Cyrus, king of Persia, is invincible, and is responsible for the downfall of Babylon.
They also probably presuppose that Cyrus has already entered the city as conqueror and has issued his decrees permitting the deportees to return and rebuild their temple. This view of Cyrus was possible only after he had deposed his sovereign Astyages of Media in 550 B.C. and had gone on to conquer the Lydian kingdom in 547 B.C. He entered Babylon in 539 B.C.

The Neo-Babylonian Empire, more accurately its Chaldean Dynasty (626–539 B.C.), was coming apart from its own internal weakness and from the incursions of Cyrus. Its current (and last) ruler, Nabonidus (555–539 B.C.), did not even reside in Babylon, preferring instead the oasis of Teima where he fostered the cult of the god Sin of Harran in preference to Marduk of Babylon. Stories of his madness later circulated. Belshazzar his son ruled for him in Babylon. Nabonidus' neglect of the national god Marduk had deeply alienated the powerful priesthood of Babylon who threw their support to Cyrus.

The priesthood may even have been responsible for the view of the Persian king incised upon the famous Cyrus Cylinder as the favorite of Marduk: "He [Marduk] pronounced the name of Cyrus, king of Anshan, declared him (lit.: pronounced [his] name) to be (come) the ruler of all the world. . . . Marduk, the great lord, a protector of the people/worshipers, beheld with great pleasure his (i.e. Cyrus') good deeds and his upright mind (lit.: heart) (and therefore) ordered him to march against his city Babylon."[1] Second Isaiah shared the same sentiments as the Cylinder regarding the divine choice of Cyrus. The prophet, however, cast the king in a characteristically Israelite image: he was the powerful wind of the storm god Yahweh. "He [Cyrus] has made them [the nations] like dust with his sword, / like driven chaff with his bow. / He chases them, he blows on unscathed, / by road on foot he does not go."[2] "I stirred up [as wind] one from the north, he came; / from the rising of the sun he called him by his name, / He has trampled rulers like clay, / like a potter treading clay."[3]

The Exile, or Babylonian Captivity, was a time of great suffering. It was also, paradoxically, a time of great literary creativity. That Exile is reckoned from July 586, when Jerusalem and the Tem-

---

1. *ANET*, 315. The entire passage is worth reading since it illustrates the Babylonian style and ideas that influenced Second Isaiah.

2. Yahweh's wind of punishment that once blew against Israel (40:7–8) now blows against kings standing in the way of Cyrus (cf. 40:24; 41:2–3 and 25, where "stir up" is the stirring up of wind).

3. 41:25. Cyrus is the instrument of Yahweh's creating here as he is in the passages, cited in the previous footnote, on the wind. Both wind and molding clay were metaphors for divine creation. Cyrus is the human agent of Yahweh's cosmogonic victory.

ple were destroyed and the second of the three deportations[4] took place, to October 539, when Cyrus entered Babylon and enabled the Judahites to return home. The devastation of the Exile ought not to be minimized. Israel had lost the ordinary symbols of peoplehood in the ancient Near East: the land which its God gave and protected and the Temple where its God dwelt. In spite of the devastation, however, there are hints that the Judahites in Babylon began to prosper relatively soon; they came to own property and to run their own religious affairs. Religious and intellectual life continued. Jeremiah preached to the Exiles. Ezekiel taught in Babylon from 597 to at least 571. Job may well have been written at this time. Anthologies of the prophets were edited. The Deuteronomistic History, originally written in the period of expansion from 621–609, was re-edited to take account of exilic realities.[5] And the greatest monument of all, the Pentateuch, was put together by priests quite near the time of Second Isaiah. Though the latter two works were edited for the most part from already existing material, their editings were by no means scissors and paste jobs. Both works show a fresh and consistent perspective, as well as exceptional sensitivity to the exiles' plight. Second Isaiah in the 540's and 530's spoke then to a community that was alert and fully capable of appreciating his condensed argumentation and of considering his call to action.

One reason that the Babylonian Exile failed to smother the voices of Israelite thinkers and poets was that threats of the loss of their land and even exile had already been experienced by the people. From the beginning Israel learned how precarious was their grip upon it. The first chapter of the Book of Judges describes an arduous and gradual conquest; unconquered pockets of Canaanites reminded them of their partial hold. The Philistines moved at will in Israel until the organized strength of Saul and David put an end to their forays. The Aramaean city-states threatened constantly in the ninth century. With the rise of the Neo-Assyrian Empire (935–612) and its western campaigns Israel for the first time came face to face with an invincible East Semitic empire. When Tiglath-Pileser (745–728) em-

---

4. At least two other major deportations took place, one in 597 and the other in 582.

5. We follow the view on the editing of the Deuteronomistic History of F. M. Cross, *Canaanite Myth and Hebrew Epic* (Cambridge: Harvard, 1973), 274–89.

barked on his first western campaign in 743–738 against the states of Syria-Palestine, Israel's and Judah's hold on the land was seemingly at the pleasure of a foreign king. Israel and Judah regularly paid tribute to Tiglath-Pileser and to his successors, Shalmaneser V (726–722), Sargon II (722–706), and Sennacherib (705–682). Assyrian pressure and internal corruption proved too much for Israel, the wealthier northern state. Capping a process of annexation of Israel's territory, the Assyrians finally took the capital, Samaria. Sargon claimed to have exiled 27,290; the northern state ceased to exist. Judah alone remained, a small client state of an Empire fully capable of destroying it. It enjoyed only one period of freedom and expansion, from 627–609, the interim between the death of Assurbanipal, the last effective Assyrian king, and the rise of Babylon under Nebuchadnezzar. Destruction of the capital city and exile in 586 were not therefore totally unprecedented. When Second Isaiah began to speak, Israel had not been truly master of its affairs for nearly two centuries.

Dependence upon the empires, first Assyrian, then Babylonian, had left its mark upon Israelite politics and prophecy during the two centuries before Second Isaiah. In politics, the constant shadow of the superpower typically provoked factions within the government, one urging cooperation with the Eastern power to the point of paying tribute, the other urging resistance through alliances with Egypt and other neighboring states. Prophets during the two hundred years record the power struggle within the governing class. Interruptions in the exercise of imperial power such as occurred while a new Assyrian or Babylonian king was eliminating pretenders or when a new empire appeared on the horizon, were attentively studied by the governing class.

The prophets were no less attentive than the governors; they believed that Israel's God Yahweh controlled all earthly empires for the benefit of Israel. Second Isaiah, in the best tradition of empire watching, read Cyrus in the way that Isaiah of Jerusalem had read the Assyrian king almost two centuries before, in Isa 10:5–19, and in the way that Jeremiah had read Nebuchadnezzar in 25:1–14, i.e. as an instrument of Yahweh. Only Cyrus was not this time one who punished but one who rescued. In fact, for Second Isaiah Cyrus em-

41; 2-3

bodied the storm wind of Yahweh which was to defeat Babylon and make possible the people's return to Zion. He was a storm wind like the storm wind that defeated Pharaoh in the first Exodus.[6] The same *storm wind* wind that once enabled Israel to pass through the hostile sea now enabled them to pass through the hostile desert.

What effect Second Isaiah's counsels to return to Zion had upon the exiles we do not know. A very large number chose not to move from their relatively prosperous situation. By the 540's, the exilic community was largely second-generation. They evidently preferred owning property and slaves in Babylon to returning to ruins and fields of uncertain ownership. A significant number did go back, however, taking advantage of the edict of Cyrus reversing the Babylonian policy of deportation.[7]

The intellectual vitality of the literary circles who edited and wrote the literature should not mislead us into thinking that the exiles as a group were confident and shared national goals. One good *audience* index of the temper of the people is the statements attributed to them. These show inertia and passivity. Second Isaiah had a difficult *X* audience.

The following sentiments, all recorded by exilic authors, show a passive and despairing acceptance of things as they must be:

> My situation is hid from Yahweh,
>   my case escapes the notice of my God.   *(Isa 40:27)* ✓

> But Zion said, "Yahweh has abandoned me,
>   my Lord has forgotten me."   *(Isa 49:14)* ✓

> Can spoil be taken from the warrior,
>   can captives escape from the victor?   *(Isa 49:24)* ✓

---

6. The storm wind, an appropriate weapon of the storm god whose traits are found in portraits of Yahweh, appears in old accounts of the Exodus, e.g. Exod 15:7, 8, 10; Ps 77:16–20. For Cyrus as the embodiment of Yahweh's wind, see note 3 and the commentary under 41:2–3.

7. Versions of the edict appear in Ezra 1:1–4 and 6:1–5. On their authenticity, see E. Bickerman, "The Edict of Cyrus in Ezra 1," *JBL* 65 (1946), 247–75.

> Destroyed is my endurance,
>> my expectation of Yahweh.   *(Lam 3:18)*

> The fathers have eaten sour grapes,
>> the children's teeth are set on edge.   *(Ezek 18:2)*

> Our bones are dried up, and our hope is lost,
>> we are utterly cut off.   *(Ezek 37:11)*

The three maxims that Second Isaiah cites do not question the existence of Yahweh (mere existence of the deity was not generally questioned in the ancient Near East) but his intention (40:27 and 49:14) and his ability (49:24) to save his people. People who live by such maxims have given up the will to survive as separate. The judgments and the feelings underlying such popular sayings are the target of the prophet's oratory. He has to demonstrate Yahweh's intention and ability to save Israel. He must show, in other words, that Yahweh "lives."[8] To prove Yahweh's *intent* to save, Second Isaiah shows that the night of exile was part of a continuum of darkness-light intended from the beginning by Yahweh. Even in the night phase, the intent to save was there. He makes use of the night-day sequence of Isa 8:16–9:7, as is suggested by the commentary on 50:1–51:8. To prove Yahweh's *ability* to save the exiles, he shows that Babylon the oppressor is without real power and cannot protect itself against Cyrus; its gods are as inert as their statues.

For Israel to overcome its deadening passivity, it must do more than change its mind; it must act. It will never come to see that its God, Yahweh, lives until it lives, acts. More precisely, it must engage in the very act whereby it came into being, the Exodus-Conquest, the creation. Hence to demonstrate Yahweh's intent and ability to save, Second Isaiah pleads with Israel to act. Only an Israel in action, an Israel that leaves Bablylon and returns to Zion, can demonstrate fully the intent and power of Yahweh to save Israel. The mood of the audience, its passivity and despair, has shaped the prophet's message.

---

8. "To live" applied to God means "intervene actively," to be "obviously present." See the article *"ḥāyâ"* in *TDOT* 4.338–39.

II. THE PROPHETIC TRADITION

By the time of Second Isaiah Israelite prophecy was almost a half-millennium old. A tradition had been established regarding the prophet's role in Israelite society, and regarding the contents and form of the prophetic message. One cannot understand the ancient context of Second Isaiah without a close look at the prophetic tradition.

The traditional role of the prophet in the Israelite social fabric is not easy to determine, in spite of the renewed interest in the topic in recent years.[9] The prophetic books are mostly anthologies of speeches. The speeches themselves, and the first and third person narratives that are included in some of the prophetic anthologies, do not provide sufficient information for a satisfactory history of prophecy in Israel. Scholars are agreed, however, that prophecy and monarchy are corollary institutions; the first prophet, Samuel, appears with the first king, Saul, ca. 1020. Indeed many scholars believe that those chapters in Samuel that deal with the rise of monarchy in Israel, 1 Samuel 1—2 Samuel 5, were early redacted by a prophetic group. Prophecy as a social institution, distinct from the literary tradition of prophecy, existed strictly speaking only when there existed the correlative social institutions of kingship and temple.

Perhaps the most instructive passages in the Bible for the prophet's *role* are contained in 1 Samuel 8–15. These chapters, now incorporated into the Deuteronomistic History of the late seventh and mid-sixth centuries, were part of an old history of the origin of the royal office and its transfer from Saul to David written from a prophetic perspective. Samuel in 1 Samuel, especially in chapters 1–15, is depicted in that great transition as the last in the line of judges and the first in the line of prophets. In keeping with the biblical habit of presenting a phenomenon already fully developed in its first manifestation, Samuel is the complete prophet. He does grandly the prophetic tasks that later prophets will routinely do. Samuel anoints Saul as

---

9. An admirable starting point for the study of the social role of the prophet is Robert R. Wilson, *Prophecy and Society in Ancient Israel* (Philadelphia: Fortress, 1980).

king, then rejects him to anoint David in his stead. His acts prefigure later prophets' legitimations and rejections, or at least criticisms, of kings. He declares holy war against the Amalekites in 1 Samuel 15, his declaration presaging later prophets' oracles against the nations. He insists that the old Mosaic tradition still holds, even under the king, in 1 Samuel 12.[10] In a word, the prophet checked and balanced the power of the king and of the royal administrators that was potentially destructive of the venerable Mosaic covenant. He represented to Israel, either in the person of the king or directly to the people, its ancient traditions, both legal and narrative. The last point, that the prophet was custodian of the narrative traditions, has been underrated by modern scholarship; it warrants further discussion.

Modern emphasis upon the prophets as proclaimers of the divine will, as speakers of the ancient law, has obscured their related role as interpreters of the national story. Samuel, the paradigmatic prophet according to the prophetic history incorporated into the Deuteronomistic History, exemplifies the prophet as interpreter of the national story. Samuel's great speech in 1 Samuel 12, a fine example of prophetic reinterpretation of the national story, is good evidence that prophets were interpreters as well as proclaimers. Second Isaiah's reinterpretation of the national story has good prophetic precedent.

1 Samuel 12 is a speech in which Samuel gathers the people to rebuke them for their rejection of governance by judgeship and their adoption of kingship. Dennis McCarthy has pointed out how the Deuteronomistic author has utilized old traditions to make of Samuel's speech an interpretation of the new monarchy.[11] The historical details are carefully selected to show Yahweh has always rescued his people from their enemies, even in Canaan when enemies equivalent to the Philistines (the present danger) had been repulsed by the divine hand. In vv. 7–12, he reviews the history, selecting and omitting details that make his point.[12]

---

10. I am indebted here to the general approach of F. M. Cross, *Canaanite Myth and Hebrew Epic*, 219–27.

11. *Treaty and Covenant* (Rome: Biblical Institute, 1978), 206–21.

12. In translating this text, I have followed in the main the text critical judgments of P. Kyle McCarter, *1 Samuel* (AB 8; Garden City: Doubleday, 1980), 209–12.

And now, present yourselves. I shall enter into judgment with you before Yahweh. I shall recount to you all of Yahweh's gracious acts which he did for you and for your fathers. When Jacob went to Egypt, the Egyptians oppressed them, and your fathers *cried out* to Yahweh. Yahweh *sent* Moses and Aaron and brought out your fathers from Egypt and settled them in this place. But they forgot Yahweh their God and he sold them into the hand of Sisera, the commander of the army of Hazor, and into the hand of the Philistines, and into the hand of the king of Moab, and they fought against them. Then they *cried out* to Yahweh and SAID, "We have sinned! For we have abandoned Yahweh and served the Baals and the Astartes. And now, rescue us from the hand of our enemies and we shall serve you!" And Yahweh *sent* Jerubbal and Bedan and Jepthah and Samson and rescued you from your enemies round about and you dwelt in safety. And when you saw Nahash the king of the Ammonites come against you, you SAID to me, "No, but a king shall rule over us!"

In the above historical recital taken from the speech, Israel's enemies attack three times. The first time, the Egyptians are the attackers, Israel *cries out* and Yahweh *sends* rescuers who bring the people to a secure dwelling in the land. The second time, Israel is attacked in the land. Israel *cries out* and Yahweh *sends* judges who again bring Israel to dwell securely in the land. Since the second attack is caused by Israel's sins, Israel *says,* confesses, it has sinned. The third attack is the attack of the Ammonites described also in 1 Samuel 11. Here Israel does not *cry out* to Yahweh, does not *say* it has sinned. It *says* instead that human kingship is the answer to its problem. The little recital is rhetorically tailored to the purposes of the whole speech. It shows that Israel's demand for a king is a substitute for its crying out to God for rescue, and for confessing its sins.

In the entire speech, of which vv. 7–12 are only a part, Samuel undertakes to "redeem" Israel's faithless choice of a king by integrating the king into the framework of the Mosaic covenant. The king as well as the people is subject to the blessings and curses (vv. 13–15). All, king and commoner alike, are to fear the Lord under pain of annihilation (vv. 24–25). Samuel has accomplished a major work of interpretation and he has done it largely through narrative. He has brought the monarchy under the ancient tradition, both legal and narrative. V. 23, "As for me, far be it from me that I should sin before Yahweh by ceasing to pray for you and teach you the good and right way," sums up the prophetic task for the future, and aptly describes what Samuel has just done.

By the time of Second Isaiah, the king, the royal administrators, the priests, scribes, the landed gentry, had all ceased to function as institutional figures among the exiled Judahites. These institutional figures had defined the prophetic "office" insofar as they represented the society in which the prophet worked. The prophet too receded as a recognizable figure in the social landscape. Though the traditional role was changing during the lifetime of Second Isaiah, the prophetic literary tradition, understood as the style and especially the message, remained alive and vivid. We turn now from the role of the prophet to the literary tradition.

In this book we propose that there was a unity to the prophetic tradition greater than generally supposed by modern scholars. We propose that there was basically a single narrative which can be called the national story. That story existed in two ideal types, one "historic" and the other "cosmogonic." The distinction between the two types depends upon the relative prominence of the human and divine actors and of the earthly and heavenly perspective. The cosmogonic version, in which Yahweh battles directly sea or desert (infertility) and leads the people out of the grasp of these hostile forces to his sacred precincts, is represented (adapted of course to Israelite monotheism) in such old traditions as Exodus 15; Deuteronomy 32:7–14; Psalms 74:12–17; 77:12–20; 89:5–37; 114. The ideal historic version, which gives prominence to humans such as Moses, Aaron, Pharaoh and his army, Joshua, or the people, is familiar to us from the prose accounts of the Pentateuch and from some Psalms—78, 135, 136. In reality, there is interpenetration of the two ideal types; historic details are found in the mainly cosmogonic types and, to some extent, vice versa.

Ancient Near Eastern stories existed in versions. The story of Gilgamesh is a good example. A recent study traces the growth and combination of versions of the story over centuries.[13] In the West Semitic world of the second millennium Baal's acquiring of kingship is told in two versions, one in which his enemy is Sea, and another in which his enemy is Death. Written copies appear to be transcriptions of a particular oral performance of a story. One of the Ugaritic texts ends with the colophon: "Written by Elimelech the Shabnite. Dictated by Attani-puruleni, Chief of Priests, Chief of (Temple)-herdsmen. Donated by Niqmadd, King of Ugarit, Master of Yargub, Lord of Tharumeni."[14] Versions abound where composition and transmission are customarily oral and where recording them on clay tablets is laborious and the speciality of palace and temple. Differences in narrative detail, omission or insertion of incidents and of characters, were expected in oral performances. The plot of the story was a given, but variations were allowed, even valued. The story of Israel's becoming Yahweh's people in Canaan also existed in versions. Our reduction of the multiplicity of versions to two ideal types is, of course, artificial, but it does allow us to classify with greater ease.

The writing prophets generally prefer the *historic* type, the Exodus-Conquest, in preference to the *cosmogonic* type. "Hear this word that Yahweh has spoken against you, O people of Israel, against the whole family which I brought up out of the land of Egypt" (Amos 3:1), is only one of several citations of the Exodus-Conquest in the Book of Amos, the first of the writing prophets, around 750 B.C. The major reference in Amos to the Exodus-Conquest, 2:9–16, will be discussed in detail below. Hosea, a decade or two after Amos, retells the story in 9:10–14; 11:1–15; 13:4–8, among other places. First Isaiah is generally judged to make little or no use of the Exodus-Conquest tradition, preferring instead the traditions of Zion and of David.[15] It is questionable, however, whether all references to the Exodus-Conquest can be denied to the prophet and, further, whether the so-called Zion and David traditions in First Isaiah are truly dis-

---

13. Jeffrey Tigay, *The Evolution of the Gilgamesh Epic* (Philadelphia: University of Pennsylvania, 1982).

14. *ANET*, 141.

15. G. von Rad has stated with special sharpness the complete disjunction between the Exodus traditions and those relating to Zion and to David in his *Old Testament Theology* (New York: Harper, 1965), 2.147–75. He is not untypical.

tinct from the Exodus-Conquest traditions.[16] Jeremiah refers to the Exodus-Conquest in the commission narrative in chapter 1 which imitates the call of Moses, and in the new covenant passage in 31:31–34. Ezekiel comments extensively in 20:1–44 on the national story. Second Isaiah, like his predecessors, retells the national story. He differs from them, however, in his easy movement between the historic and cosmogonic types, and in holding each in exquisite balance. A beautiful example of his holding of the two types together is 43:16–21.

> [16]Thus says Yahweh,
>   the one who makes a way in Sea,
>   a path in the Mighty Waters,
> [17]the One who musters chariot and horse,
>   all the mighty army.
>   They lie prostrate, no more to rise,
>   they are extinguished, quenched like a wick.
> [18]Recall no more the former things,
>   the ancient events bring no longer to mind.
> [19]I am now doing something new,
>   now it springs forth, do you not recognize it?
>   I am making a way in the wilderness,
>   paths[17] in the desert.
> [20]The wild beasts will honor me,
>   jackals and ostriches.
>   For I have placed waters in the wilderness,
>   rivers in the desert,
>   to give drink to my chosen people,
> [21]the people whom I have formed for myself,
>   to narrate my praiseworthy deeds.

---

16. I hope to show in a forthcoming article that Isaiah's Zion traditions are part of the national story in its cosmogonic type. They describe the idyllic life in Yahweh's holy precincts. The David traditions are also related to the cosmogonic type, part of the installation of the king at creation. See for a provisional sketch, "Psalm 89: A Lament over the Davidic Ruler's Continued Failure," *HTR* 73 (1980), 35–47.

17. We read *ntybwt* for MT *nĕhārôt* with 1QIsaᵃ and according to sense.

The prophet has fused the Exodus-Conquest and the cosmogonic version of the account of Israel's origins (vv. 16–17) and, as corollary, the "new event" of a new Exodus-Conquest and new cosmogony. The enemy this time is Desert, as it was Sea in the old times. The power of Sea or Desert to keep Israel from the land is broken. In each case the hostile force is tamed by means of the path that is laid through it.

The important question, of course, is the function of the national story in the prophets. Its function in the prophets is like its function in pre-prophetic literature, expecially the old Epic composed in the Tribal Period (ca. 1250–1020 B.C.), and later written down as the Yahwist and Elohist versions. The Epic told how Israel went from servitude to Pharaoh in Egypt to servitude to Yahweh in Canaan. Other traditions might supplement the core story, either by way of preface, as in the primeval history (Genesis 1–11) and the patriarchal stories (Genesis 12–50); or by way of insertion within, as the legal material; but the movement from Egypt to Canaan provided the permanent backbone. True, the J-E account of the Conquest seems to be missing from the present Pentateuch, but the complete scheme, the Exodus-Conquest, is preserved in pre-exilic poetry such as Ps 78:42–55. The promise of land in the patriarchal stories and in the promises in Egypt (e.g. Exod 3:17) argue strongly that the old Epic originally contained the Conquest before the exilic editing that produced the Pentateuch and Deuteronomistic History.

The story defined who Israel was by narrating the people's origins. The ancient Near Easterner, who did not have a sharpened modern sense of historical development, typically thought of a phenomenon as fully realized in its first manifestation. The impress of God's shaping hand was freshest in the first appearance. Thus the essence of man and woman and the nature of marriage are best seen in their first appearance in Gen 2:4–3:24. In this sense, the origin of a reality explains its essence.

The origin of Israel is an act; its essence is dramatic. In the historic type of the national story, Yahweh rescues the people from slavery to Pharaoh in Egypt through Moses and brings them to serve him in his land of Canaan. In the cosmogonic type, Yahweh tames the power of sea or desert that keeps his people from his land. Yah-

weh removes the hostile power by making a path for Israel to walk
safely through to his land. The last mentioned aspect of the national
story in its cosmogonic type—the passage through a tamed sea or desert to the holy sanctuary—needs further explanation before we continue with the function of the story in Israel's recital. It is
particularly important in Second Isaiah.

That Yahweh enabled Israel to pass through the Red or Reed
Sea to safety on the other side is a familiar motif from such poems as
Pss 114; 77:16–20; 136:13–15. Ps 77:19 is clear: "Your way was
through the Sea, / your path through the Great Waters." It is important to observe further that in some pre-exilic poetry Yahweh leads
his people through the hostile desert as well as through the hostile
sea. Ps 136:16, "to him who caused his people to walk through the
desert," seems to match v. 14, "he caused Israel to pass through its
midst (i.e. sea)." More persuasive (and more indisputably pre-exilic)
is Ps 78:52-53: "He set his people moving like sheep, / he guided
them, a flock, in the desert, / He led them in safety so that they were
unafraid, / as for their enemies the sea covered them."

The clearest pre-Deutero-Isaian text on the desert as the hostile
power from which Israel must be rescued is Deut 32:10-13, part of
an historic recital in the Song of Moses.

> He (Yahweh) found him (Israel) in the desert land,
>   in chaos (tōhû), in a howling wilderness.
> He surrounded him, he cared for him,
>   he protected him like the apple of his eye.
> Like an eagle that stirs up his nest,
>   over his nestlings hovers,
> he spread out his pinions, he took him,[18]
>   he bore him on his wings.
> Yahweh alone led him,
>   no strange god was with him.

---

18. The *RSV,* "spreading out its wings, catching them, / bearing them on its pin-
ions," is misleading. It suggests that the adult eagle (really the Griffon Vulture) is
teaching its young to fly by dropping them in the air and then swooping down to catch
them. The picture rather is like Exod 19:5: Yahweh rescues the people from danger by
picking them up and flying them to his sacred precincts.

He made him sit on the high place of the earth,
   he ate the produce of the field.

When Second Isaiah speaks of Yahweh leading the people through the desert, he is making use of traditions like those cited above.

Israel defined itself by reciting the story. When Israel told its story, especially in the self-conscious solemnity of liturgy in the Temple court (which expressed in a special way the sacrality of the land), it actualized itself as Yahweh's people in an intense way. Whether it recited a version of the historic or the cosmogonic type, it experienced Yahweh as the one who brought it into being by the process of defeating its enemy and of bringing it to himself in his land. In modern terminology the historic type is called *redemption* and the cosmogonic type is called *creation*. They are however the same event—the emergence of Israel as a people before Yahweh.

It is highly significant that the pre-exilic prophets do *not* tell the national story in the same way as the old Epic told it. The old Epic, reflected in the old poetry and in J-E before its exilic redaction and truncation, ended with Israel safe in the land. The pre-exilic prophets had heard Yahweh issue a decree of destruction in the heavens against Israel. The prophet could only announce the imminent destruction.

> This is what the Lord Yahweh showed me. There was a basket of figs (*qayiṣ*). Yahweh said to me, "What do you see, Amos?" I said, "A basket of figs (*qayiṣ*)." Yahweh said to me, "The end (*qēṣ*) has come upon my people Israel. I will not forgive them any more." (Amos 8:1–2)

The ending of the traditional story is changed in the prophetic interpretation. Israel is to encounter Yahweh now not in his land but in his act of judgment. Israel may, after the judgment, regain possession of the land, but only that part of Israel who have accepted the judgment. And future land possession takes second place in prophetic preaching to the imminent punishment. The task of the prophet was to prepare Israel for the new ending of the story, for the encounter with Yahweh in an act of war rather than in the land.

Amos 1–2 offers an excellent example of prophetic retelling of the story. After indicting a succession of neighboring states for violations of the divine will, Amos turns to Israel and confronts it with violations of the divine law. His justification for the sentence is couched in narrative.

Thus says Yahweh,
For three transgressions of Israel,
 for four, I will not revoke the punishment.
Because they sell those whose cause is just,
 the poor for a pair of sandals.

[Vv. 7–8 describe violations of the rights of the poor and the
 holiness of the sanctuary.]

Yet I destroyed the Amorite from before them,
 tall as the cedar,
 strong as the oak.
I destroyed his fruit above,
 his roots below.
I brought you up from the land of Egypt,
 I led you through the wilderness forty years,
 that you might inherit the land of the Amorites.
I raised up some of your sons to be prophets,
 some of your young men to be nazirites.
Is this not so, Israelites?"
 —oracle of Yahweh.
But you made the nazirites drink wine,
 you ordered the prophets, Do not prophesy!
I will now press you down in your place,
 as a cart full of sheaves presses down.
Flight shall fail the swift,
 the strong shall not retain his strength,
 the warrior shall not save his life.
The bowman shall not hold his ground,
 the swift of foot shall not escape,
 nor the horseman save his life.
Even the stout of heart among warriors,
 shall flee away naked in that day.   *(2:6–16)*

"That day" in the last verse is a day of holy war.[19] Yahweh turns as warrior against Israel as he did against the Amorites, to expel them from the land.

The pre-exilic prophets translated the divine decree of destruction against Israel into an historical scenario to clarify Yahweh's act of judgment. According to the scenario, Yahweh attacks Israel using a human army as his instrument. After the punishing attack there will be a restoration, a renewed remnant. Amos' description of the divine attack through an earthly army has been cited above.

Isaiah and Jeremiah, both influential upon Second Isaiah, offer explicit scenarios of divine judgment through military attack by an army, the punishment of the avenging army for exceeding its mandate by unnecessary cruelty to Israel, and the restoration of Israel. Isa 1:21–26(27) is a beautiful, chiastically arranged poem describing the divine attack and the restoration of the holy city. Isa 10:5–19 (probably continued in 14:24–27) is the clearest Isaian text on the prophetic scheme, and is explicitly alluded to by Second Isaiah, in 44:24–45:13. Cyrus in the later passage is commissioned just as the Assyrian king was, and 45:9–13 quotes the dialogue of 10:15.

Jeremiah at first spoke only of the enemy from the north as Yahweh's avenging instrument. Later he names Nebuchadnezzar, king of Babylon (605–561), as the agent of punishment. Jer 25:8–14 *v̄. ᵍ.* shows the scheme of destruction through an (unwittingly) commissioned pagan king and the punishment of the same king for exceeding the mandate.

> Therefore thus says Yahweh of hosts: Because you did not obey my words, I am now sending to take all the peoples of the north—oracle of Yahweh—and Nebuchadnezzar, the king of Babylon, my servant, and to bring them against this land and its inhabitants, and against all the nations round about. . . . And those nations shall serve the king of Babylon seventy years. When the seventy years are over, I will

---

19. At the time of Amos, Israel expected that Yahweh would always go in front of its armies against the enemy. They assumed that "that day" would be, therefore, a day of light, a day of victory. The famous passage in Amos—"Alas, those who desire the day of Yahweh. . . . It is darkness, and not light"—expresses well Amos' understanding of Yahweh the just warrior coming against Israel.

punish the king of Babylon and that nation and the land of the Chaldeans for their sins.

Jer 29:10 is explicit about restoration: "When seventy years of Babylon are over, I will visit you and fulfill for you my gracious word, to bring you back to this place."

Ezekiel also agrees with Jeremiah. He looked for a restoration of the people, purified by the Exile, to a purified land. Jeremiah and Ezekiel believe Israel comes into being as Yahweh's people *in the land*. Jer 29:10–14 is clear on the point and it echoes other texts of Jeremiah. And Ezekiel envisions Israel restored in its land in chapters 40–48.

Second Isaiah adopts the pre-exilic prophetic scenario and its presuppositions, except that he turns it around. For him, the judgment of Yahweh was not future; it had already occurred in the destruction of the Temple and the deportation of the people. Israel had suffered the consequences of its action, had "borne its sins." A new divine decree had been issued: " 'Comfort, comfort my people,' says your God" (40:1). The instrument of consolation was a human king, as was the instrument of punishment in pre-exilic times. Cyrus in Second Isaiah functions like the Assyrian king in First Isaiah and the Babylonian king in Jeremiah.[20] The foreign king, Cyrus, rebuilds the Temple and brings back the people. He is a mirror image of the earlier avenging king.

One element of the national story, Israel's profound orientation to Yahweh *in the land*, became for Second Isaiah the core of his preaching. In the cosmogonic version Israel was led through the sea or the desert to Yahweh's shrine, often a mountain. In the historic type, Israel was rescued from Pharaoh and settled in Canaan. Jeremiah and Ezekiel had expressly conceived divine forgiveness as a regrouping of a chastened people upon the soil of Canaan. To Second Isaiah, Israel becomes truly Israel when it engages in the act of returning, when it leaves Babylon and crosses the desert to Zion. The

---

20. The view of some scholars that Cyrus is the servant in Second Isaiah, or was until the prophet became disappointed in him, fails to apprciate the analogous function of the pagan king in First and Second Isaiah.

prophet's conviction that Israel must seize the moment flashes out in his exhortations.

> Go forth from Babylon,
> flee from Chaldea.
> Announce with jubilant voice,
> declare it.
> Publish the word
> to the ends of the earth.
> Say, "Yahweh has redeemed
> his servant Jacob!"
> They thirsted not
> when he led them through parched places.
> Water from the rock
> he made flow for them.
> He split the rock,
> there flowed out water.   *(48:20–21 and cf. 52:11–12)*

Second Isaiah is steeped in the old prophetic literary tradition though he presents it with striking originality. He accepts the pre-exilic prophetic revision of the national story whereby Israel encountered Yahweh not in secure possession of the land but in an act of judgment. For him, however, the judgment has occurred and has led to the dissolution of Israel. He goes back, therefore, to the original story of the emergence of Israel in the old poetry: a people was led out of subservience to false gods in Egypt and brought to the service of the true God Yahweh in Canaan. That story is to be played again with only a slight change in terms: Babylon for Egypt and Zion for Canaan. Second Isaiah goes back to the old Epic. Israel, if it is obedient to the word of God, will dwell securely in the land. Thus does Second Isaiah show his mastery over the tradition.

III. The Context of Modern Scholarship

The third component of the context of Second Isaiah is modern—the web of assumptions that modern biblical scholars have made about the prophet and his books and the methods of analysis they have used in the last two centuries. It is important to recognize how profoundly the last two hundred years of critical scholarship have affected our understanding of the book. Second Isaiah is unique in the Bible in that its very existence as a work separate and distinct from that of eighth century Isaiah[21] only began to be recognized in the last quarter of the eighteenth century. Because the recognition of chapters 40–55 as distinct from chapters 1–39 is owed so totally to critical scholarship, modern interpretation of the chapters has reflected with unusual sensitivity successive trends of that scholarship.

The last two hundred years of investigation of the book can, for convenience of discussion, be divided into four stages. Each of the stages is marked by the gaining of a seminal insight and (what is often forgotten) is marked at the same time by a distortion resulting from the overstatment of discovery or from rigidity of application of a method. The following paragraphs dwell on the distortions rather than on the gains because the distortions have often gone unexamined. I do not wish to appear ungrateful to the scholars assessed below; we all stand in their debt. I must, however, justify the approach and method used in this book. To note some of the limits of competing approaches is part of that justification.

Apart from suspicions regarding the eighth century composition of chapters 40–55 on the part of such medieval scholars as Ibn Ezra (d. 1167), Jewish and Christian scholars alike up to the late eighteenth century saw no reason to doubt that the whole book of Israel was written by one and the same man, Isaiah of Jerusalem who lived, as the opening verse has it (1:1), "in the days of Uzziah, Jotham, Ahaz, and Hezekiah, kings of Judah." The oracles that mention events later than the eighth century, like those in Isaiah 15–16; 21:1–10 and 40–66, were seen by the eighth century prophet in vision, according to the traditional view. This monolithic view among critical scholars did not survive the skepticism of the Enlightenment.

The first scholar to gather together the doubts beginning to be expressed about a single Isaiah and to give them wide publicity was Johann Gottfried Eichhorn (1752–1827) in his much used *Einleitung*

---

21. First Isaiah's material is contained in chapters 1–39, though by no means all the chapters are attributed to the eighth century prophet by modern critical scholarship.

in das Alte Testament.[22] Most of the sixty pages he devotes to Isaiah are spent on proving that the Book of Isaiah was not written by one person but is rather an anthology of material dating from the eighth century to post-exilic times. He persistently battles "the reigning view" that all the chapters are the work of Isaiah. He shows in detail that chapters 15–16, 21 and 40–52 cannot be from Isaiah of Jerusalem, emphasizing how different the chapters are in language, ideas, and historical background from the undoubtedly First Isaian chapters. Of chapters 40–52 he writes: "In the series of oracles just mentioned the Babylonian exile is the general setting; the poet speaks as if he lived in exile, as if he spoke to the exiles who in the delay of their return to the homeland doubt whether the promise of their old prophets will be fulfilled. Must not the author of the consoling tradition contained in them have lived in the exile?"[23] His final conclusion is strongly stated: "Over time this collection of oracles came to be regarded as a work whose author was Isaiah alone. For people soon forgot—apparently only a few had ever known—that he had grown from the compilation of completely diverse oracles spoken by the most diverse prophets of the most diverse times."[24]

Eichhorn's arguments against the unity of Isaiah did not end the discussion. It took nearly a century and a half of insistence upon the differences between chapters 1–39 and 40–55 to bring about general acceptance of a sixth century date for the latter chapters. Victory, however, brought a distortion. For with the correct view that a sixth century author wrote chapters 40–55 there went the almost inevitable, but false, corollary—that chapters 40–55 are utterly different from chapters 1–39. The result has been that the important analogies between the two complexes have not been given their due importance, and Second Isaiah's sense of himself as a self-conscious disciple of First Isaiah has likewise been downplayed. Among the important analogies between the two prophetic books are: the enemy king is the agent of punishment (10:5–19) or restoration (especially 44:24–45:13); Mount Zion is the sole place of divine dwelling and

---

22. I used *Einleitung in das alte Testament* (Leipzig: Weidman, 1803), volume 3 on the prophets. The first edition was 1780–83.

23. Ibid., 69. Translation is my own.

24. Ibid., 114–15. "He" apparently refers to the figure of Isaiah in the tradition. Note how strong is the emphasis that various parts of the book are unrelated.

disclosure (2:1–5 and 50:1–51:8 with commentary); the true disciples know the movement of divine process from darkness to light (8:6–9:7; 30:8–14). These and other important continuities between the two books were lost sight of, victims of the long battle to prove how different each prophetic author was from the other.

The distinctiveness of chapters 40–55 could be taken for granted by Bernhard Duhm (1847–1928), the most important shaper of twentieth century views on Second Isaiah through his *Die Theologie der Propheten* (1875), his Isaiah commentary (first edition in 1892), and his popular *Die Profeten* (1916). He marks the second stage. Duhm has been justly praised for his commentary which remains indispensable.[25] His judgment (made already in the book of 1875) that the four poems of the servant of Yahweh were an insertion into chapters 40–55 is, however, a major distortion. The judgment illustrates well the uncritical use of the then dominant method of literary criticism. His characterization of the servant songs in his commentary (*sub* 42:1–4) merits quotation both because of his conclusions and his methodology.

> The poems of the servant of Yahweh, 42:1–4; 49:1–6; 50:4–9; 52:13–53:12, immediately impress one by style, by lofty vocabulary, by the regularity of verses and strophes. In vocabulary and ideas they depend quite closely on Second Isaiah's writing but relate only partially to their context; their removal leaves no gap. The same, it is true, can be said of many passages. Their main point, the idea of the servant of God, is also not unknown in Second Isaiah, but it is handled by him in a completely different way. For the latter, Israel as it exists is the servant of Yahweh—chosen, protected and destined by Yahweh for a glorious future though at the present time blind and deaf, imprisoned and plundered, a worm, despised by the Gentiles, sinful. On the contrary, the hero of these poems is set over against the people, is innocent, Yahweh's disciple daily enlightened by him, called to a mission to the people and to the Gentiles

---

25. He demonstrated successfully that chapters 56–66 are distinct from chapters 40–55. In his 1875 book he had not yet arrived at that conclusion.

and attending to his call in complete calm. In sharp contrast to Second Isaiah who is clearly audible and summons the whole world to his audible announcement, his voice is not heard in the street. Also he suffers, but as a Jeremiah and a Job have suffered, from the abuse of unbelievers among his own people, from the leprosy with which Yahweh has struck him, and not, like Israel, from foreign oppressors. . . . The author of these calm, profound and unsensational poems cannot, because of temperament, be the same as the thundering, lively Second Isaiah. He appears to have written after the Book of Job and before the Book of Malachi, in any case not in the Exile. One can argue whether the poems once existed as a separate book or were composed only for the Book of Second Isaiah. Because of certain additions, however (cf. 42:5–7; 50:10, 11), the first assumption is more likely. These additions seem to derive from the author who inserted the poems in Second Isaiah's work in the first place. He inserted such passages where sufficient space was available, on the margin, between sections or spaces on the paper, without taking account of the Deutero-Isaian context. The first poem, 42:1–4, with the addition of vv. 5–7, obviously interrupts the close connection between 41:21–29 and 42:8ff.[26]

The methodology implied in the excerpt—namely an alertness to inconsistencies within a passage that suggest different sources, as well as reconstruction of the pre-history of those sources—is a reminder how closely Duhm stands to his colleague and friend Julius Wellhausen and to that scholar's projects and methodology.[27] Scholars of the period were fascinated by the Pentateuch much more than they were by the prophets. Much attention and energy were devoted to identifying and sorting out the several sources of the Pentateuch, the Yahwist (J), the Elohist (E), the Priestly (P), and in reconstruct-

---

26. *Das Buch Jesaia* (4th ed.; HAT 3.1; Göttingen: Vandenhoeck & Ruprecht, 1922), 311. Translation is my own.

27. See further on Duhm's relation to Wellhausen and his methodology, H.-J. Kraus, *Geschichte der historisch-kritischen Erforschung des alten Testaments* (2nd ed., Neukirchen-Vluyn: Neukirchener Verlag, 1969), pp. 275–83.

ing their pre-history. The contemporaries of Duhm correctly saw
that ancient versions of Israel's legal and narrative traditions had
been combined into the Pentateuch in a complicated and lengthy
process. It was their task to become sensitive to the redactional process that brought the diverse strands together—inconsistencies, repetitions, breaks in the progression of thought, uneven vocabulary—
and to make hypotheses on how the sources came to be combined.
This was the original environment of *Literaturkritik* or, more accurately, discernment of sources.

Analytical instruments are designed for the material they ana-
lyze. For the multi-layered Pentateuch the proper procedure was to
look for signs of sources and then to reconstruct the history of the
sources. What was proper in the Pentateuch was not, however, nec-
essarily proper for the prophets. One could not simply assume that
Second Isaiah was composed like the Pentateuch. In short, Duhm
and many who followed in his steps did not keep in mind that *Literaturkritik* is a procedure found useful for the Pentateuch; it is not a
pure method universally applicable to every kind of biblical literature.

Though voices of protest had all along been raised against the
excision of the servant passages,[28] Duhm's position has prevailed.
The "Servant Songs" as a separate group have become a fixture in
biblical theology, providing New Testament students in particular
with a convenient set of passages for comparison. A similar fate has
befallen Daniel 7, which speaks of the Son of Man. Because of its
New Testament relevance, it has been taken from its context and
studied in isolation.

The four passages on the servant were not the only passages
Duhm excluded on the grounds of interruption of context: several
passages on the making of statues have been judged non-Isaian on
the same grounds. Isa 46:6-8 and 44:9-20 were deemed intrusive in
their contexts and yet to have sufficiently shared vocabulary and
concepts to constitute a "source." The other substantial passages on

---

28. One well known opponent of opposing the servants in the "songs" to the servant elsewhere in Second Isaiah is Otto Eissfeldt, *The Old Testament: An Introduction*
(New York: Harper, 1965), 340–41. The first edition of this influential volume was in
1934. Another is Harry Orlinsky, *Studies on the Second Part of the Book of Isaiah*
(VTSup 14; Leiden: Brill, 1967).

statues, 40:18–20 and 41:5–7, were deemed originally to have been part of chapter 40 and included 40:17–19 + 41:5–7 + 40:20. The reasoning here is the same as in the servant songs; it is assumed that the book is composed of pre-existing material like the Pentateuch, that these sources can be identified by signs such as inconsistencies of language and ideas, and that the history of the sources can be tentatively arrived at.

Duhm's attribution to a hand other than Second Isaiah's of the servant songs and the satires on statues not only illustrates his approach; it also shows the tendency of Duhm and his followers to assume that Second Isaiah's thought is monolithic; what is not "logical" is judged to be added by another. The possibility, for example, that the servant can be Israel in the "non-servant" passages and yet in other passages stand over against the people is excluded on *a priori* grounds. Ancient Near Eastern narrative logic, its love of dramatic contrast[29] and the interplay of facets of a single issue, is denied. Passages are rearranged without any textual warrant.

The third stage in the history of modern study arrived with the application of form criticism to Second Isaiah. Hermann Gunkel (1862–1932), the founder of form criticism, correctly affirmed that "types in the literature of an ancient people play a much greater role than today and that the individual personalities of authors, which in modern literature are, or appear to be, everything, in antiquity step back in a manner quite bewildering to us."[30] He focused therefore on the literature rather than on the author, and especially on the genre of the literature, cataloguing typical features. He also was interested in the *Sitz im Leben,* the situation in the life of the people in which the genre developed. Gunkel had the genius to know which books particularly suited his new method—Genesis and Psalms, for each of which he wrote a superb commentary. Genesis is popular literature reflecting the life of the folk in themes, composition, and transmission. The Psalms, as literature for public worship, are highly stereotyped. Form criticism, with its sensitivity to genres and their origin in the life of the folk, elucidates these books brilliantly. The method

---

29. For examples of dramatic contrast in the idol passages, see my "The Function of the Idol Passages in Second Isaiah," *CBQ* 42 (1980) 450–64.

30. Cited in Kraus, *Geschichte,* p. 361.

is less satisfactory for Second Isaiah. With its emphasis on the typical and the recurrent, it slights authorial individuality and originality. With its quest for the origin of the genres in the life of the people, it can ask the wrong questions when an individual is composing with consciously new intentions.

Form criticism, despite its shaping in types of literature quite different from Second Isaiah, is the most widely used method today in the study of chapters 40–55. Hugo Gressmann in 1914, Ludwig Köhler in 1923, and Joachim Begrich in 1938 all applied form criticism to the prophet. Begrich's concise book especially remains perennially influential upon a whole generation of contemporary scholars, among whom Claus Westermann is the most prominent.[31]

Form criticism, the reckoning with the genres of the literature and their attendant motifs and vocabulary, of course has to play a prominent role in the study of the prophet. This book constantly applies it, as a glance at the commentary makes clear. But it is abused easily. The most damaging result of the overdominance of form criticism on Second Isaiah is the determination of the length of units by considerations from genre rather than from the logic of the particular piece. The result has been the atomization of the chapters into small units on the assumption that the poem's length is coextensive with the form that is used.[32] The poet is thus stripped of his ability to write long and complex orations. The message is drained of subtlety and persuasive force.

The fourth and final stage in the history of modern scholarship on the prophet is the application of rhetorical criticism, generally associated with the commentary of James Muilenburg in *The Interpreter's Bible* in 1956. Twelve years after his commentary, Muilenburg

31. His *Isaiah 40–66: A Commentary* (Philadelphia: Westminster, 1969), a translation of a 1966 German original, is perhaps the most widely used commentary on Second Isaiah in English.

32. Roy Melugin, *The Formation of Isaiah 40–55* (*BZAW* 141; Berlin: De-Gruyter, 1976), is an example of a book in which considerations of genre play a preponderant role in determining boundaries of units. Yehezkel Kaufmann, *The Religion of Israel* (translated and abridged by Moshe Greenberg; London: Allen & Unwin, 1961), is particularly eloquent in criticism of the tendency, pp. 359–60. See also his *The Babylonian Captivity and Deutero-Isaiah* (History of the Religion of Israel IV.1,2; New York: Union of American Hebrew Congregations, 1970), 75–76.

offered some theoretical considerations on the method in his presidential address to the Society of Biblical Literature.

> What I am interested in, above all, is in understanding the nature of Hebrew literary composition, in exhibiting the structural patterns that are employed for the fashioning of a literary unit, whether in poetry or in prose, and in discerning the many and various devices by which the predications are formulated and ordered into a unified whole. Such an enterprise I should describe as rhetoric and the methodology as rhetorical criticism.[33]

True to his later theory, Muilenburg's commentary is sensitive to compositional techniques—word play, assonance, rhythms—which reveal conscious rhetorical development. He does not allow form critical considerations to determine the length of a unit, but assumes "the poet," as he frequently calls Second Isaiah, to incorporate several genres within a single composition. Muilenburg is exceptionally appreciative of the spontaneous and the creative in Second Isaiah, and elucidates this aspect of the chapters with insight.

The rhetorical approach is not, however, free of problematic tendencies, some of which appear in the 1956 commentary. Scholars have criticized his neglect of form criticism.[34] More basic is the tendency (in the commentary proper rather than in the introduction of it) to divorce the text from its context, i.e. both the relation of each text to the literary tradition and to historical events. His constant reference to Second Isaiah as a poet is symptomatic. The main interest is the medium, rather than the environment understood as literary and intellectual tradition and as history.

What was only a tendency in Muilenburg, a tendency generally in dialogue with other approaches, can become in less skilled hands a genuine flight into aestheticism. It is worth quoting a noted English

---

33. "Form Criticism and Beyond," *JBL* 88 (1969), 8.
34. C. Westermann in his "Sprache und Struktur der Prophetie Deuterojesajas," in *Forschung am alten Testament* (Theologische Bücherei 24; Munich: Kaiser, 1964), 106–10; and R. Melugin, *Formation*, esp. pp. 7–10.

scholar, Walter Jackson Bate, regarding a similar tendency in English studies.

> The movement loosely called Romanticism produced many important and valuable results, but in its late, extreme form (by the 1880s and 1890s when [university] departments were founded), its emphases on the purely personal and idiosyncratic helped to cut off approaches in the arts to large public issues and values; and the result was a strong leaning toward aestheticism—which means, in effect, that interest focuses less on literature and the arts as a total interplay of mind and experience than on the special *medium*—the texture, the tonal qualities, the image-patterns, the semantic associations: in short, the formal qualities. This tendency is necessary up to a point. But it can become exclusive and thin itself out in the process. Carried far enough, it can lead to an ignorant bias against all kinds of writing other than what Aristotle calls the "mimetic forms" (poetry, prose, fiction, and drama) and a neglect of great intellectual prose—history, oratory, philosophy.[35]

The application of rhetorical criticism to Second Isaiah is the fourth and last step in the two hundred year process of discovery and delineation. This book is indebted to Muilenburg's approach which appreciates rhetoric and allows sustained development of thought. I differ in seeing Second Isaiah as an orator rather than a lyric poet. I emphasize the interpretation and persuasion that is going on in the speeches; they are designed to persuade people to go back to Zion. Muilenburg is inclined to leave the poet's vision unconnected to a concrete proposal.

The history of recent scholarship on Second Isaiah is a history of losses and of gains. Proving that chapters 40–55 were different from chapters 1–39 obscured the fact that Second Isaiah was himself a disciple of the eighth century master. Literary criticism, betraying the signs of its birth in pentateuchal analysis, excised the servant passages and the idol passages. Rhetorical criticism, ushered in as a self-

---

35. "The Crisis in English Studies," *Harvard Magazine* 85.1 (Sept.–Oct. 1982) 48.

conscious method by James Muilenburg in the 1950s and 1960s, and helped along by the "New Criticism" of English studies about the same time, occasionally displays its potential to divorce the text from its context of literary tradition and history, and to become mere aestheticism.

This book attempts to learn the lessons of history. We assume that chapters 40–55 are separate from chapters 1–39 but that Second Isaiah is a self-conscious disciple of First Isaiah, entrusted with his writings. Form criticism, understood not as the reconstruction of ideal forms but rather as sensitivity to genres and their conventions, is used throughout. Lastly we are in sympathy with rhetorical criticism but we attempt to relate it to the total environment of prophetic tradition, audience, and historical events.

Chapter Two

THE SHAPING OF THE MESSAGE

Second Isaiah reckons that Israel is living in the third stage of restoration in the traditional scenario of (1) punishment of Israel through a human agency, (2) Israel's bearing of the punishment, and (3) the restoration of the remnant. Restoration for him can only come about through a renewal of the Exodus-Conquest, the cosmogony, by which the people march to the holy land and rebuilt city. Such a summary, however, is only of limited value in guiding the modern reader through Second Isaiah. The core of his thought he often only alludes to; he counts on the tradition to be so deeply ingrained in his audience's heart and head that mere hints suffice for the whole to be called up. Further, oratory, by definition occasional and practical, is resistant to summary. A summary of the thought alone tends to prescind from the modes of its expression, hence to divorce style from content. A method of exposition other than summary must be found.

Fortunately the oratory itself provides a means of synthesis that does not pull apart expression and argument. Second Isaiah in all his speeches makes persistent use of five contrasted concepts which both shape and advance the thought and are themselves his major points. The contrasts, or polarities, are: the first and last things, Babylon and Zion, Israel and the nations, Yahweh and the gods (or their images), the servant and Israel. They will serve as the outline of the chapter.

I. PRELIMINARY QUESTION OF UNIT LENGTH. RHETORICAL CLUES

Before we turn to the message, a difficult preliminary question must be resolved: what are the original boundaries of the individual speeches? As already mentioned in the Introduction, determining the length of the units is crucial to the interpretation. Are the speeches of sufficient length to develop ideas, or are they so brief as to supply only a series of images and brief scenes? The manuscripts do not preserve the original units. No scholarly consensus exists today about the appropriate method of discovering the boundaries nor about the resulting nature and number of the units. Yet the number of units is vital and virtually predetermines a scholar's interpretation. To conclude, for example, that there are many units and to do so chiefly from considerations of genre leads one to concentrate upon the relation of the genre in Second Isaiah to instances of the same genre in earlier literature rather than on the coherence of the thought *within* Second Isaiah.[1] On the other hand, to conclude that there are few units (for example, twenty-four with Muilenburg or in our view seventeen) leads one to concentrate upon rhetoric and compositional techniques that unify long composition.

No single method suffices for discerning the original boundaries of compositions unified by so many different means: by strophic patterning,[2] by techniques such as word play, by repetition of sounds, by rhymes, and—especially befitting oratory—by coherent and compelling argument. The unity of each passage will be discussed in detail in the commentary. In this section we only offer some general observations on Second Isaiah's strophic patterning and other techniques of composition.

Strophic pattern is an important structuring device. The third speech, 41:1–42:9, is an example of one type of parallel structure.[3]

---

1. The tendency is strongly represented in influential studies such as those by J. Begrich, *Studien zu Deuterojesaja* (Theologische Bücherei 20; Munich: Kaiser, 1969 [German original 1938]); C. Westermann, "Sprache und Struktur bei Deuterojesaja," *Forschung am alten Testament* (Theologische Bücherei 24; Munich: Kaiser, 1964), 92–170; A. Schoors, *I Am God Your Saviour: A Form-Critical Study of the Main Genres of Is. XL-LV* (SupVT 24; Leiden: Brill, 1973).

2. We recognize that the word strophe is a term describing Greek, not Semitic, poetry. It designates "patterned recurrence," a phenomenon of Semitic poetry. It seems wisest to retain the term. See further M. Coogan, "A Structural and Literary Analysis of the Song of Deborah," *CBQ* 40 (1978), 11–12.

3. For detailed analysis of the structure, see the commentary and my "The Function of Idol Passages in Second Isaiah," *CBQ* 42 (1980), 450–64.

	A. 41:1–20	B. 41:21–42:9
Summons to trial	41:1, 5–7	41:21–22b
Legal questioning of nations/their gods	2–4	22c–29
Verdict on nations and Israel	8–20	42:1–9

Chapter 48 also is composed in two matching sections, vv. 1–11 (39 cola) and vv. 12–21 (37 cola).

	A. 48:1–11	B. 48:12–21
Hear, O Jacob	vv. 1–2	vv. 12ab
Link between divine word and deed	3–8	12c–16
Yahweh's zeal accomplishes all	9–11	17–19

Chapter 49 has 55 cola in vv. 1–13 and 52 in vv. 14–26. In the first section the disbelief of the servant is overcome; in the second, the disbelief of Zion. In chapter 55 the invitation to the banquet, with variations, is issued twice in vv. 1–5 and 6–11.

Isaiah 55 and 40:12–31 illustrate another type of pattern, proportional strophes.

40:12–17	18 cola	55:1–5	18 cola
18–24	22	6–11	21
25–31	26	12–13	9

More usual is approximate equality of cola in strophes.

44:24–28	20 cola	54:1–5	21 cola
45:1–7	28 (v. 8 is probably extra-stanzaic)	6–10	20
9–13	20	11–27	22

Of the other rhetorical techniques only a brief sample will be given here. The Hebrew poetic tradition offered a rich variety of devices to its authors—chiasm, assonance and alliteration, end rhymes, various parallelisms—and Second Isaiah made use of them all. To point out all of them is beyond the aim of this book which stresses rather the coherence of the thought. The reader is referred to Muilenburg's valuable discussion in his commentary.

One device must, however, be pointed out since it provides clues to the structure of some poems—*word play*. In 41:5–13, repetition of the same vocabulary in two juxtaposed scenes—"to fear," "the ends of the earth," "to say," "to help," "to be strong, grasp," is ironic, to show how the nations talk to one another and to their silent passive gods (vv. 5–7) while Yahweh addresses a multitude of consoling words to a silent Israel (vv. 8–13). In chapter 48, *qārā,* "to call," in the first section (vv. 1–11) occurs three times in the sense "to call oneself, to be known as," with Israel the subject, and occurs three times in the second section, vv. 12–21, in the sense "to call, to summon," with Yahweh as the subject. The usage underscores the thought of the poem.

II. THE FIRST OF THE POLARITIES: FIRST AND LAST THINGS

The previous section contained instances of parallel structure in the speeches. Structural parallelism is but one instance of a larger phenomenon which pervades biblical thought and expression. The most widely recognized and pervasive parallelism in the Bible is that of verse lines: "When you walk, your step will not be hampered; / when you run, you will not stumble" (Prov 4:12). In a manner different from an English poet who often aims at a single statement memorable by its compression, the Hebrew poet generally aims at the dramatic interplay, the reverberation, between two (sometimes three) similar statements. The Semitic hearer was used to expect poetic meaning in the movement between the two (or three) rather than in the static polish of a single utterance.

What is true for parallelism of verses holds true also for larger assemblages: parallelism between scenes and parallelism between actors. This aspect of biblical style is sometimes overlooked and needs elucidation. A good example of parallelism of scenes is Proverbs 9:1–6 + 11 // 13–18.[4]

A.	B.
1 Wisdom has built her temple,	13 The foolish woman shouts,
She has erected her seven pillars.	Untaught, she knows nothing.
2 She has slaughtered her meat,	14 And she sits at the door of her temple,
She has mixed her wine.	Upon a throne at the high place of the city.
Yes, she has set her table.	15 She calls to the passers-by,
3 She has sent out her messengers,	Those who walk straight ahead.
She calls out at the high point of the city.	16 "Whoever is simple, let him turn aside here,
4 "Whoever is untaught, let him turn aside here,	And the one lacking understanding, she will teach him.
the one lacking understanding, she will teach him.	17 Water stolen is sweet,
5 Come, eat of my food,	Food (gotten) in secret is pleasant."
And drink the wine I have mixed.	18 But he does not know that the rephaim are there,
6 Abandon folly and live,	In the depths of Sheol are the ones she has invited.
And walk in the path of insight.	
11 For with me your days will be made many,	
And the years of your life will be increased."	

In one panel Dame Wisdom invites the untutored youth to her banquet, and in the other Dame Folly invites the same youth to her banquet. The author wants his hearers to let the invitation of one woman be heard against the background of the other's call. Claim and counterclaim make the statement.

Parallel actors in a scene, the second of the two extended devices mentioned above, also occurs. In Exod 1–15, Pharaoh is portrayed by the Priestly redactor as the "god" of Egypt, demanding hard service of the Hebrews, interfering with Yahweh's blessing of progeny (by killing the males) and of land (by refusing to allow them to leave Egypt); he will not allow them to worship their God. Pharaoh with his magicians, and Yahweh with Moses and Aaron, are portrayed in parallel, locked in combat for possession of the Hebrews. The plagues are assaults in the holy war. Yahweh wins and brings his people to serve him in his land.

---

4. For justification of the excision of vv. 7–10, see my "Proverbs IX: A Suggested Ugaritic Parallel," *VT* 25 (1975), 304, n. 8.

Second Isaiah makes use of the device of parallelism in opposing the old Exodus-Conquest to the new act by which Israel comes into new existence. The old national story, recited in liturgical assembly or on less solemnly sacred occasions, grounds the national identity. In the Exile, however, the master story in its classic form ceased to be credible. For the story ended with Israel dwelling secure in its God's land, but Israel was in Exile! A new interpretation was called for.

Second Isaiah declares the Exodus-Conquest is still valid, except that Israel is now in "Egypt" at the beginning of its journey, not at the end. The old story had it that Israel was living in Yahweh's land and the people were to be grateful and loyal to Yahweh alone amid the seductions of Canaan. Second Isaiah taught that Israel was again in Egypt (Babylon) and that the people were to journey to Zion. To describe this historical analogy, Second Isaiah uses the terms "first and last" and "Babylon and Zion."

First and last has more than one meaning in Second Isaiah.[5] The terms can be a simple merism for eternity, as in 41:4: "I, Yahweh, the first, / with the last I am he!" "First" also refers to the divine word that precedes and announces the divine deed as divine because predicted by the god. This usage in Second Isaiah occurs in trial scenes where Yahweh questions the gods on their divinity, i.e. their power to predict and then fulfill the prediction: 41:22–23 and 42:9; 43:9–13;[6] 44:6–8; 45:20–21. Chapter 48 explores almost in a theoretical way the same link between prediction and deed. It is the third meaning of first and last, however, that is directly relevant to Second Isaiah's historical analogy mentioned above, and this is found in 43:16–21 and 49:9–13. In 43:18, "the former things" (*ri'šōnôt*) is paired with "ancient events" (*qadmōniyôt*) in the context of the Exodus-Conquest and cosmogony. The same contrast informs 46:9, "Remember the first events, from olden days," where Yahweh carries Israel to safety.

Though there are many more references to the Exodus-Con-

---

5. For a survey of discussion and a brief discussion of the relevant passages, see Carroll Stuhlmueller, *Creative Redemption in Deutero-Isaiah* (Rome: Biblical Institute, 1970), 135–168.

6. V. 12ab makes it certain that the witnessing is to Yahweh's power. See the commentary.

quest in Second Isaiah than these two texts, we will begin with them because of their explicitness.

> [16]Thus says Yahweh,
>   The one who makes a way in the Sea,
>   a path in the Mighty Waters,
>   [17]the one who musters chariot and horse,
>   all the mighty army.
>   They lie prostrate, no more to rise,
>   they are extinguished, quenched like a wick,
>   [18]Recall no more the former things,
>   the ancient events bring no longer to mind.
>   [19]I am now doing something new,
>   now it springs forth, do you not recognize it?
>   I am making a way in the wilderness,
>   paths[7] in the desert.
>   [20]The wild beasts will honor me,
>   jackals and ostriches.
>   For I have placed waters in the wilderness,
>   rivers in the desert,
>   to give drink to my chosen people,
>   [21]the people whom I have formed for myself,
>   to narrate my praiseworthy deeds.

The entire speech, 43:9–44:5, from which the above has been excerpted, appoints Israel as the witness of the only God who speaks and then acts unopposed according to his word. In vv. 16–21, Yahweh declares he will act to overcome the sterility of the desert ("I am now doing something new") that keeps Israel from reaching its land. The new act is validated by its similarity to the old act. Yahweh

makes in the Sea a way	places in the wilderness a way
in the Mighty Waters a path	in the desert paths
(v. 16)	*(v. 19)*

---

7. We read *ntybwt* with 1QIsa[a], and according to sense, in place of MT *nhrwt*.

Israel, in this interpretation of the story, is in the position of crossing over the desert to Zion. They are at the first act of their story. Isaiah 46 makes the same statement. Yahweh has carried Israel ("carrying" is a verb used in some accounts of the Exodus-Conquest) and will always carry. "Remember the first events, from olden days" (v. 19). Yahweh will again carry Israel to Zion.

Historical analogy between the Exodus-Conquest and the present situation is much more pervasive than the occurrences of the words "first and last." The analogy is basic to several speeches and in fact constitutes important evidence that the speeches are lengthy and serious. In 40:3–5 the taming of the desert by roads over which Yahweh will lead his people alludes to the national story. Isa 41:7–20 and 42:13–16 similarly allude to the story, especially the cosmogonic type, in speaking of the future taming of the desert for Israel's sake. Both 48:20–21 and 52:11–12, in calling upon Jews to flee Babylon, implicitly state that the journey is a new Exodus from Egypt. Chapter 49 puts the commission of the servant in the categories of Moses' commission. Further, the chapter describes the work of the servant as leadership in the wilderness and apportionment of the land (vv. 8–12)—the work of Moses (and Joshua). The great prayer of 51:9–52:12 that Yahweh destroy the enemy and bring his people to Zion begs God to renew today the great deed that brought the people to Zion. Finally Isa 55:12–13 makes the trees that line the desert highway equivalent to the twelve stones of the highway through the Jordan in Josh 4:6–7; they both commemorate the miraculous crossing through hostile powers.

III. THE SECOND POLARITY: BABYLON AND ZION

The second polarity, Babylon and Zion, also is part of the great analogy between the first Exodus-Conquest and the situation in Second Isaiah's day. As noted, 48:20–21 and 52:11–12 are exhortations to the Jews to flee Babylon using the vocabulary of the first Exodus. Zion is mentioned in the opening vision: "Go up to a high mountain, / O Zion, messenger of good tidings. / Raise your voice aloud, / Jerusalem, messenger of good tidings. / Raise your voice, do not be afraid, / say to the cities of Judah: /'Here is your God!' " (40:9). The disconcerting image of Mount Zion ascending a high mountain to proclaim joyously the coming of her God is only partly explained by its personification as messenger.[8] The rising of Zion is also intended as complement to the downfall of Babylon in chapter 47: "Get down, sit in the dust, / Fair Maiden Babylon. / Sit upon the ground—there is no throne— /Fair Chaldea. . . . Sit in silence, go into the darkness, Fair Chaldea" (47:1, 5). The explicit contrast between Babylon and Zion begins with the command given to Cyrus in 44:28 (cf. 45:13) to rebuild Jerusalem: "(Yahweh) saying to Cyrus, 'My shepherd! / He will do my pleasure, / will say of Jerusalem, "Let it be rebuilt; / let the Temple be refounded." ' "

From this speech forward to the end, from 44:24–45:13 to chapter 55, Zion is in the foreground. Babylon as mirror image to Zion gives depth to many scenes. In the speech on the necessity of rebuilding Zion, 45:14–25, the ruin of Babylon (chapter 47) provides contrast. The gods are carried from doomed Babylon in chapter 46, in contrast to Yahweh carrying Israel to Zion. Zion is restored as queen and mother in 49:14–26 but widowhood and childlessness are visited upon the tyrannical queen Babylon in chapter 47. Assurance of husband and children is given to Zion also by the two rhetorical questions that begin 50:1–52:8. Chapter 48 declares that Yahweh is to be worshiped only in Zion (v. 2), that Cyrus has broken the power of Babylon (v. 14), and hence Israel is to flee Babylon (vv. 20–21). Chapters 54 and 55 are also about Zion, chapter 55 being especially insistent that Zion is the goal of a procession that originates in Babylon.

The Zion-Babylon polarity makes clear that Zion is the only place where Yahweh can be worshiped. Babylon is the land of the tyrant and is full of false gods. The old tradition sometimes put the Exodus-Conquest in just those simple geographic antipodes. The Israelites served Pharaoh in Egypt and served Yahweh in Canaan; the land itself seems to express the dominion. For Second Isaiah Babylon was polluted and about to be destroyed. Zion is the restored, rebuilt sacred city, the goal of the procession from darkness. Babylon is the

---

8. Isa 2:1–5, a text mined more than once by Second Isaiah, speaks of the word of Yahweh coming from Zion.

land of captivity and of subservience to false gods. Zion is the land of freedom and of true worship and divine manifestation.

IV. The Related Polarities: Yahweh and the Gods, Israel and the Nations

The next two polarities are likewise closely related: Yahweh and the gods, Israel and the nations. For clarity in presentation, a preliminary word needs to be said about the first polarity by itself, Yahweh and the gods, before it is discussed in relation to the polarity with which it is frequently paired.

Very significantly, the theme of Yahweh versus the gods (or the images which represent them to their human worshipers) appears chiefly in trial scenes: 41:1–42:9; 43:9–44:5; 44:6–23; 45:14–25 (vv. 20–21). In addition, 40:12–31 and chapter 48 bear on the question. Form critics are divided about the *Sitz im Leben* of the trial scenes. Are they literary reflections of everyday court practice or of liturgical origin? There is no question, however, about Second Isaiah's mastery in demonstrating dramatically through them that Yahweh is God alone. The trial is not about existence but power, the ability of a god to control events on earth. One event in particular is under investigation: the victorious course of Cyrus which has made him the most powerful king in the East. Which god or gods are his heavenly patrons, powering his victories? In accord with the legal custom of the time, Yahweh is presiding judge and prosecuting attorney; he both questions and renders the verdict.

The proof of Yahweh's divinity is not, as might be inferred from a first reading of texts like 41:21–23, 25–26; 44:7, and chapter 48, that he is the only God who predicts events before they happen. The proof of divinity is suggested by the texts from Ugarit (an ancient city in present-day Syria), of the late second millennium and reflective of the same general culture as Israel. In these texts, the god Baal demonstrates his power over the gods and attains the insignia of kingship, the temple, by vanquishing threats to cosmic order which the other gods were not able to quell. His deed of removing threats to world order constitutes creation in the common West Semitic understanding of the term. The superiority of the storm god in the world of the gods, effected through his act of creation, is stated with exceptional clarity in the Akkadian epic *Enuma elish.*[9] It is reasonable to expect that Yahweh in Second Isaiah will prove his superiority, or kingship, in the common ancient Near Eastern way: by establishing the world through defeat of enemies of the world. This is in fact what the biblical texts say: Yahweh is the sole deity because he alone creates, he alone leads the Exodus-Conquest.

The single human personage mentioned in the trial scenes, Cyrus the Persian king, also suggests that Yahweh is the only deity because he is powerful to create. It is always in connection with cosmogony that Cyrus is named or alluded to, as in the embodiment of Yahweh's mighty wind in 41:2–3.

> [2]Who roused from the east the graciously chosen one,
>   summoned him to his service?
> Who delivers nations into his hands,
>   treads upon kings?
> He makes (them) like dust with his sword,
>   like driven chaff with his bow.
> [3]He chases them, he blows on unscathed,
>   by road on foot he does not go.   *(41:2–3)*

Cyrus embodies also Yahweh's power to create, as a potter molds clay.

> He has trampled rulers like clay,
>   like a potter kneading clay.   *(41:25)*

He also builds the sacral city and temple, the task of the gods in ancient Near Eastern creation accounts.[10]

> Cyrus . . . will say of Jerusalem, "Let it be rebuilt; let the temple be refounded." (44:28)

---

9. It is possible that the conflict between Marduk, the storm god, and Tiamat, Sea, originated in the West Semitic world. See Thorkild Jacobsen, "The Battle between Marduk and Ti'āmat," *JAOS* 88 (1968), 104–8.

10. See Arvid Kapelrud, "Temple Building, a Task for Gods and Kings," *Orientalia* 32 (1963), 56–62.

Cyrus is also the king anointed at the act of creation in 45:1–6[11] and
48:14–15. Yahweh proves his divine rank by overcoming his enemies, the enemies of cosmic order, the enemies of human community
and hence of Israel.

If prediction by itself does not constitute proof of divinity, what
is the function of the divine word in the trial scenes? It occurs frequently.

> [21]Present your case, says Yahweh,
>   set out your evidence,
>   says the King of Jacob.
> [22]Let them draw near and let them tell us
>   what is about to happen.
> The first things—what are they?
>   Tell us that we may consider them,
>   that we may know their outcome.
> Or, what is coming, inform us.
> [23]Tell us what is coming in the future,
>   that we may know you are God   *(41:21–23)*

> [25]I roused one from the north, he came;
>   from the rising of the sun he called (him) by name.
> He has trampled rulers like clay,
>   like a potter kneading clay.
> [26]Who told this from the beginning that we might know it,
>   from of old that we could say, "It is true"?
> No one told, no one announced,
>   no one heard your utterance.   *(41:25–26)*

> [7]Who like me can announce,
>   can tell and so prove himself my equal?
> Who announced from of old events yet to happen,
>   told them what is to take place?   *(44:7)*

---

11. In Psalm 89 the king is appointed as the regent of God over the newly created
world.

The point in all these passages is that nothing can hinder Yahweh's word; to speak without fear of opposition is the mark of a king.

> For I know that Yahweh is great,
>   our Lord is greater than all the gods.
> Whatever Yahweh pleases he does,
>   in the heavens and on the earth,
>   in the waters and on the deeps.[12]

The word of Yahweh in these passages therefore is the announcement of his victory, the cosmogony through taming of hostile forces. His victory is unopposed; only to announce it is to bring it about.

As stated at the beginning of Section IV, the polarity of Yahweh and the gods is incomplete without the closely related fourth polarity, Israel and the nations. It is important to note first an ancient presupposition about heaven, the world of the immortal gods, and earth, the world of mortals. Though the biblical focus is generally on the world of human beings rather than upon the world of the gods (thus differing from much of the polytheistic religious literature), it presupposes the ancient Near Eastern dualism of heaven and earth. Heaven and earth are clearly distinguished yet are in parallel. What the gods decide will inevitably take place on earth. As an aspect of the dominance of the heavenly world, the rank or prestige of a god in the assembly of the gods has to be reflected on earth. Earthly recognition consistitutes a god's glory. Mortals sought to "give god glory," i.e. to recognize and acknowledge the power and prestige the god enjoyed in the heavenly world.

The ordinary means by which the god in heaven became present to his or her worshipers on earth in the ancient Near East was through images. An earthly image imitated by its shape the heavenly reality; it "re-presented," i.e. made the god present to the worshiper. The imitative object might be broader than a statue. A temple and its furnishings made the god's house present to the worshipers. So did the rituals which imitated and made present the ceremonies of the

---

12. Ps 135:5. The Psalm goes on to speak of creation. The reference is to the battle over chaos. See further H.-J. Kraus, *Psalmen* (4th ed.; BK 15/2; Neukirchen-Vluyn: Neukirchener Verlag, 1972) 2.897.

heavenly court. The resemblance did not need to be exact; impressionistic likenesses sufficed. The statue of a god made the god visible on earth. Its beauty and its value (from gold and precious stones) reflected the heavenly beauty and worth of the god represented. To the worshiper the material of the image was not divine; it was only a means to an end. It provided the occasion for an encounter between the god and his devotee.

However widely accepted the use of images might be among its neighbors, Israel was forbidden their use. Its aniconic tradition was ancient: "I am Yahweh your God, who brought you out of the land of Egypt, out of the house of bondage. You shall have no other gods before me. You shall not make for yourself a graven image, or any likeness of anything that is in heaven above, or that is of the earth beneath[13] or that is in the water under the earth" (Exod 20:2–4). Israel's encounter with Yahweh was through the hearing of his word. Its distinctiveness lay in that. "Then Yahweh spoke to you out of the midst of the fire; you heard the sound of words, but saw no form; there was only a voice. And he declared to you his covenant, which he commanded you to do, that is, the ten words, and he wrote them upon two tablets of stone. . . . Therefore take good heed to yourselves. Since you saw no form on the day that Yahweh spoke to you at Horeb out of the midst of the fire, beware lest you act corruptly by making a graven image for yourself, in the form of any figure, the likeness of male and female, the likeness of any beast that is on the earth, the likeness of any winged bird that flies in the air, the likeness of anything that creeps upon the ground, the likeness of any fish that is in the water under the earth" (Deut 4:12–13, 15–18).

Israel eliminated statues of Yahweh from its worship. It did not, however, eliminate every instance of the ancient Near Eastern principle of re-presentation of heavenly reality through earthly representation. The Tabernacle and the Temple are examples of imitation of heavenly dwellings. And the rites performed in them allowed the community to participate in the ceremonies of the heavenly court. During the Exile, two Israelite thinkers made daring new interpretations of earthly imaging of divine perfection—man as the image of

---

13. The image need not be anthropomorphic; it could be an animal, e.g. a serpent, which could "present" an aspect of the divine power.

God. One was the Priestly writer who composed the creation account in Gen 1:1–2:3; the other was Second Isaiah.

Gen 1:1–2:3 is the Priests's own preface to the Pentateuch
which he put together in the Exile from old traditions and from material of his own. His first chapter shows the place of man and woman in the universe.

> [26]God said,
>   "Let us make man in our image,
>   after our likeness.
>   Let him have dominion over the fish of the sea,
>   over the birds of the heavens,
>   over all the cattle upon the earth."
> [27]God created man in his image,
>   according to the image of God he created him,
>   male and female he created them.
> [28]God blessed them,
>   God said to them,
>   "Be fertile and increase,
>   fill the earth and master it.
>   Rule over the fish of the sea,
>   over the birds of the heavens,
>   over every animal that creeps upon the earth."

Claus Westermann in his commentary on these words has emphasized that they describe primarily the deed of God, not the nature
of man. That deed makes possible an intermediate creature between
himself and the rest of creation. V. 26a shows that "the special character of man is seen in his correspondence (Gegenüber) to God. The
orientation is not extrinsic to the being of man; rather man is so created that his being is defined in the orientation to God."[14] God has
made man his correspondent on earth to resemble him, to represent
him. And it is not static man and woman that represent God; they
represent him in their action, begetting progeny, gaining possession
of land, exercising appropriate dominion. The jussive and imperative

---

14. *Genesis* (BK 1; Neukirchen-Vluyn: Neukirchener Verlag, 1966), 218. The
translation is my own.

verbs, "Be fertile and increase, fill the earth and master it, rule . . ."
define "image and likeness"; man/woman is above the animals and
are to act out the blessing of propagating themselves and possessing
the earth.

Yahweh as represented on earth by humans on earth is also the
teaching in Second Isaiah. He is thoroughly traditional in his denial
that statues represent him: "I am Yahweh, that is my name; / my
glory I shall not give to another, / my renown to idols" (42:8). Yet in
the very same speech he contrasts the statues which image forth only
the inert impotence of the gods and Israel who, by traversing the desert, images forth the unique power (hence deity) of Yahweh.

The lengthy speech, 41:1–42:9, is the clearest exposition of the
idea that Israel-in-act is the image of Yahweh on earth. As is shown
in detail in the commentary, the speech consists of two matched
halves, 41:1–20 and 42:21–42:9. In each half, the nations of the
world with their gods (and the statues imaging them) are summoned
to a trial in which Yahweh is both the questioner and the judge.
They are asked what deity is granting to Cyrus, king of Persia, the
military victories that are transforming the political map of the East,
and making it possible for Israel to return to their land. The deities,
in the person of their statues, say nothing; their silence before the
great question of the age reflects their impotence in contemporary
events. The only activity is that of their worshipers who made the
"gods" and who must carry them while they are being questioned
(41:5–7, 21). The silence of the images in the face of Yahweh's questioning them about Cyrus is taken to be a sign of their nullity: "an
abomination is he who chooses you" (41:24); "Here are all of them—
nothing; / nonexistent their deeds, / wind and chaos their images"
(41:29).

In the same speech, in contrast to the gods whose inert images
represent their inertness only too well, Yahweh chooses Israel. In
each half of the poem, Yahweh addresses Israel immediately after
the gods'/images' inability to explain Cyrus, 41:8–20 and 42:1–9.
Yahweh's sudden turn to Israel in each section suggests by its position a deliberate contrast to the gods' relation to their images. In the
first address to Israel after the silence of the gods in 41:8–10 Yahweh
uses terms for Israel that the nations had used for the statues, "en-
courage," "from the ends of the earth," "help," "say." The implica-

tion is clear: Yahweh chooses to be with Israel (v. 10a), to punish its enemies (vv. 11–13), to destroy barriers to its return home (vv. 14–16), to facilitate a new Exodus-Conquest by overcoming the sterility of the desert (vv. 17–19). The climactic v. 20 is important: "that people may see and acknowledge, / observe and understand, / that the hand of Yahweh has done this, / the Holy One of Israel has created it." From Israel's march through the desert, people will see the power of its God. The people, by its activity, become the icon of Yahweh.

The conception of Israel as the icon of its God is even more visible in the second divine address to Israel in 42:1–9. Vv. 1–4 state that Israel will make known the rightness of Yahweh's case to the world. Israel is empowered to overcome primordial darkness in 42:6–7, as it had overcome the sterility of the desert in 41:17–19; both are references to the march to freedom from bondage that is soon to take place. Yahweh declares that he does not trust a statue to represent his glory (v. 8). By implication, Israel's activity, its revival as a people, shows the overcoming of chaotic darkness.[15] By its revival as a people, Israel represents Yahweh's glory to the world.

Outside of the great speech of 41:1–42:9, Israel as the reflector of Yahweh's heavenly luster is expressed most succinctly and clearly in the term "witness." Israel is called Yahweh's witness (ʿēd) in three passages, 43:9–10; 44:6–9 and 55:4–5. The clearest passage is 43:9–10, part of the speech 43:9–44:5.

[9]Let all the nations gather together,
  let the peoples assemble.
"Who among them has announced this,
  has proclaimed the former things.
Let them produce their witnesses to prove them true,
  that people may hear and say, "It is true!"
[10]You are my witnesses—oracle of Yahweh—
  my servant whom I have chosen,
so that you may know and believe in me,
  that you may understand that I am The One.

---

15. Darkness is not mere absence of light. As Gen 1:1–5 and especially Ps 104 show, darkness characterizes the world before God's word imposes order. Darkness is relegated to its proper sphere, nighttime.

Before me no god was formed,
    after me none will exist.
[11]I, I am Yahweh,
    there is no saving (god) beside me.
[12]I announce, then I save,
    I proclaim; no other god is there among you.
You are my witnesses—oracle of Yahweh—that I am God,
[13]ever since day was, I am The One.
No one can wrest (anything) from my hand,
    I act; who can stay it?

Israel and the nations are summoned to trial. The nations are to produce their witnesses, the statues of their patron deities.[16] Israel is the witness of Yahweh.

What is Israel to witness in this speech? The chiasm of vv. 10–13 (for which see the commentary) centers on v. 12ab as the main statement: "I announce, then I save; / I proclaim; no other god is there among you." Israel witnesses to Yahweh's telling what he will do and then doing it unopposed. The general principle of v. 12ab is specified in vv. 14–21: Yahweh caused the Exile and causes the new Exodus-Conquest/Creation. No one opposed his word in the First Exodus (vv. 16–17) and no one will oppose it in the Second (vv. 19–21). As noted earlier, the god wins his status as king of the gods by his cosmogonic victory over Sea and Death. By his act of victory Yahweh is known as the only God. Israel witnesses to it, not by speaking but by doing. By participating in the Exodus-Conquest/Creation the people make Yahweh's victory visible on earth.

Only an Israel obedient to the divine will can truly witness to Yahweh's unopposed power. An Israel resignedly dwelling in Babylon or Egypt—anywhere outside of Zion—demonstrates only that a once proud people had been vanquished and exiled. To be a witness, to demonstrate the victory of its God, Israel has to obey the summons to embark on a new Exodus-Conquest. Insofar as it is obedient to his summons Israel is called by Second Isaiah the servant. Properly speaking only the servant—those associated with the prophet's

---

16. Isa 43:6–9 is clear regarding the statues as witnesses.

program of return—makes the unique power of Yahweh visible to the nations.

V. The Fifth Polarity: The Servant and the People

The conception of Israel as the witness-in-action of the creation victory which proves Yahweh's sole divinity suggests the last of the great polarities, the servant and Israel. The servant is Israel obedient to the divine word. Bernhard Duhm in his book of 1875 formulated the matter well: "All Israel can scarcely be called the servant of God simply because the word of God has resided in it. It is truly the servant of God only in so far as it accepts and carries out the word consciously and willingly. We therefore understand by the term servants of Yahweh ideal Israel which has God's word and in accord with it mediates the dealings of God to Israel and indirectly to the entire world."[17] The orientation of the servant to the people, so nicely stated by Duhm, is in fact a constant of servants of Yahweh in biblical literature prior to Second Isaiah. Moses the great servant (cf. Num 12:6–8), David, and others are called servant because of the favor of God by which they exercised authority and responsibility for the people. Without the orientation to the people, it is hard to imagine what the servant's *raison d'être* might be. In insisting upon the mutuality of servant and people, Duhm was simply stating an old truth.

Unfortunately the mutuality of the Deutero-Isaian servant and the people has been underrated by the mainstream of post-Duhm scholarship. Duhm himself was partly responsible in that he sharply distinguished, especially in his commentary of 1892, between the servant of his four "poems of the servant of Yahweh" and the servant elsewhere in chapters 40–55. The former he portrayed as mysterious, even romantic: ". . . the hero of these poems is set over against his people, is innocent, Yahweh's disciple daily enlightened by him . . . his voice is not heard in the streets . . . he suffers, but as a Jeremiah and a Job have suffered, from the abuse of unbelievers among his own people. . . . The author of these lofty, profound and unsensation-

---

17. *Die Theologie der Propheten als Grundlage für die innere Entwicklungsgeschichte der israelitischen Religion* (Bonn: Adolph Marcus, 1875), 292. The translation is my own.

al poems cannot, because of temperament, be the same as the thundering lively Second Isaiah."[18]

Small wonder that scholars set out on a search to learn the name of this intriguing figure. For over half a century the search went on. In the course of it a number of kings were proposed—Hezekiah, Uzziah, Jehoiachin, Zerubbabel, even Cyrus—and not a few prophets—Isaiah of Jerusalem, Jeremiah, and Second Isaiah himself.[19] In recent years most scholars have turned their energies from trying to identify the servant to studying his function.[20] We have already argued that the distinction between an individual servant in the "songs" and Israel in the rest of the speeches is an invalid one. The distinction has been responsible for the frenetic search for the individual servant and consequently for obscuring the mutual orientation of servant and people.

Because the servant in Second Isaiah is not a private individual[21] who acts in isolation from people, his action affects the whole community intimately. The servant can stand for the people. The whole people is called to leave Babylon and to return to Jerusalem in a new Exodus-Conquest. Not all obeyed the summons. Not all realized the profound reasons why the Exile took place and consequently did not "offer their back to the smiter" (50:6), i.e. did not accept it as divine punishment. Not all were zealous for the glory of Yahweh; they did not allow themselves to be gathered as Israel so as to prove to the nations that Yahweh is a living God. Not all were willing to obey the

---

18. *Das Buch Jesaia* (4th ed.; HAT 3.1; Göttingen: Vandenhoeck & Ruprecht, 1922) under 42:1. The translation is my own.

19. Convenient surveys in English are those by C. R. North, *The Suffering Servant in Deutero-Isaiah* (2nd ed.; London: Oxford, 1956) and more briefly in his article, "Servant of the Lord, The," in *The Interpreter's Dictionary of the Bible* (Nashville: Abingdon, 1962), 4.292–94; Colin G. Kruse, "The Servant Songs: Interpretive Trends Since C. R. North," *Studia Biblica et Theologica* 8 (1978) 3–27.

20. Today many scholars would agree with Claus Westermann: "On principle, their [the songs] exegesis must not be controlled by the question, 'Who is this servant of God?' Instead, we must do them justice by recognizing that precisely this is what they neither tell nor intend to tell us. The questions which should control exegesis are: 'What do the texts make known about what transpires, or is to transpire, between God, the servant, and those to whom his task pertains?' " *Isaiah 40–66: A Commentary* (Philadelphia: Westminster, 1969), 93.

21. We speak here of the function of the servant. We propose that the servant is Second Isaiah and those who go with him in the new Exodus-Conquest.

command to return when it meant a dangerous journey home to claim property now held by others, to give up property certainly held and a position in the Babylon community. The servant embraced all these tasks, and through him Israel came to life again.

By being part of a reconstituted people that proves Yahweh's power in 42:1–9, by leading the people home and apportioning the land like Moses and Joshua in 49:1–12, by facing willingly the brunt of divine punishment in 50:4–11, and by waiting for ultimate divine upholding of their seemingly mortal peril in 52:13–53:12, Second Isaiah and his followers proved that they were the servants *par excellence*. And they continued by their actions and words to address their blind and sluggish brethren to follow their lead.

For Second Isaiah, then, true Israel will be the people who, at this dark moment when Israel has fallen back into the Egypt of bondage, do the act that pulls it back into existence, the Exodus-Conquest. Zion is the goal toward which they march. Second Isaiah differentiates among the people. One group is obedient, the servant; the other is not. But as long as that one group does return, the other group somehow comes into being. One group's faith-filled sacrifice of its reputation, goods, and safety rescues the other group from non-existence. The servant and the people are bound inextricably together.

We have looked at the major polarities structuring Second Isaiah's thought and style. We now go to a particular feature of his thought in the next chapter: creation.

Chapter Three

CREATION

Creation, it has been several times remarked, is the leading idea
in Second Isaiah. This chapter draws together comments already
made and arranges them with new material so as to make a synthetic
statement.

It is important at the beginning of any discussion about creation
to distinguish ancient and modern conceptions. In the last two centuries modern science and evolutionary thinking have come into being
and have shaped the mental habits of the industrial West. As a result
there is some confusion in modern discussion regarding creation in
the ancient Near East and in the Bible.[1] For the sake of clarity, we
use the term cosmogony for the ancient West Semitic conception and
creation for the modern, though it is not possible to be perfectly consistent.

I. Four Differences between the Ancient and Modern Conceptions of Creation

The differences in conceptualizing or, perhaps, better, of imag-
ining creation can be reduced to four: the process of creation, what

---

1. F. M. Cross has clarified the meaning of creation in Semitic antiquity by distin-
guishing between theogony, the birth and succession of the gods, especially the old
gods, and cosmogony, "characterized by a conflict between the old and the young
gods out of which order, especially kingship, is established in the cosmos." See his
"The 'Olden Gods' in Ancient Near Eastern Creation Myths," in *Magnalia Dei* (G. E.
Wright Festschrift; ed. F. M. Cross *et al.,* Garden City, N.Y.: Doubleday, 1976) 329–
38. Loren Fisher has insightfully explored some of the differences between ancient and
modern conceptions, and between varieties of ancient accounts, in "Creation at Ugarit
and in the Old Testament," *VT* 15 (1965) 313–24. A. S. Kapelrud, "Creation in the
Ras Shamra Texts," *Studia Theologica* 34 (1980) 1–11, criticizes Fisher on the basis of
his own unnuanced definition of creation.

emerges from the process, the range of the explanation, and awareness of development.

The first difference lies in the way the process of creation is
imagined. For moderns, the process is often evolutionary, and works
according to physical laws. These laws are impersonal and, under the
right conditions, can be duplicated in the laboratory. For ancients,
on the other hand, the process involved personal wills and generally
was conflictual. Typically the process was a series of dramatic acts: a
threat to the established order, a battle and a victory, a celebration of
the kingship won through the victory. Both in the Ugaritic texts of
Late Bronze Age Canaan and in the Bible (in which of course major
transpositions have taken place), the storm god (or Yahweh with
some of the traits of the storm god) tames the destructive power of
sea or death.

The conflict generally ends, not with the annihilation of the enemy, but with the relegation of the hostile force to a prescribed
sphere. Within that sphere the evil power cannot work against the established order and sometimes is even made to contribute to the
functioning of an orderly universe. In the conflict between the storm
god Baal and his enemies Sea and Death in the Ugaritic texts, the
victory of one divine being means the confinement of his foe.[2] When
Mot is in power, he confines Baal to the underworld. The same is
implied when Yam is in power. It is probable that Baal confines Sea
and Death when he comes into his power. Infertility, whether in the
form of salt sea or of death, was not annihilated but only confined to
a place where it could no longer harm society.

The Bible differs from the Ugaritic texts in that the rule of Yahweh is not subject to alternation; it is permanent. He defeats and confines unruly elements once for all. If they do return, it is because he
has willed it so. Psalm 104 illustrates how much the beauty of the
universe for the Israelite consists in the precise taming of the intrac-
table forces that had made human life impossible. The opening verses
of the Psalm depict the confinement of the previously unruly waters
to the sea.

---

2. Mot confines Baal to the underworld in *CTA* 5.1–6.2 (*UT* 67, 49). It is implied
in *CTA* 2.1 *(UT 'nt)* that Yam will confine Baal. Baal's return to life means a return of
fertility and hence the restriction of infertility.

[5](You, Yahweh,) who found (*yōsēd*[3]) earth upon its
  foundations,
  it shall not be shaken forever and ever.
[6]The deep covered it like a garment,
  over the mountains the waters stood.
[7]At your rebuke they fled,
  at the sound of your thunder they rushed away.
[8]They went up the mountains, they went down the valleys,
  to the place which you founded for them.
[9]The boundary you set they shall not cross,
  they shall never again cover the earth.

The rest of the Psalm praises God for making previously hostile primordial darkness and cosmic waters support human life. Even Genesis 1, often pointed to as an example of non-conflictual creation, parallels the dual taming of Psalm 104: on Day One primordial darkness is assigned to nighttime and on Day Two the waters are separated to form the sea.

The word of Yahweh is what makes the unruly primal forces play their assigned part in a beautiful and harmonious universe. Jer 4:23–26 shows what happens when Yahweh withdraws his word from the world.

[23]I looked on the earth, and lo, it was waste and void;
  and to the heavens, and they had no light.
[24]I looked on the mountains, and lo, they were all quaking,
  and all the hills moved to and fro.
[25]I looked, and lo, there was no man,
  and all the birds of the air had fled.
[26]I looked, and lo, the fruitful land was a desert,
  and all its cities were laid in ruins
  before the Lord, before his fierce anger.   *(RSV)*

In some texts the power of sea or desert is broken, not so much by placing them where they can no longer harm society, but by mak-

---

3. For text critical and translation problems of the opening verses, see my "A Note on Ps 104:5–9," *JBL* 10 (1981) 87–89. Note the personfication of the waters (their being endowed with will) here and in Psalms 77 and 114.

ing a road through them. Sea or desert stands between Yahweh's
people and their land.

> [16]The waters saw you, O God,
>   the waters saw you, they were convulsed,
>   yea, the deep quaked.
> [17]The clouds poured forth water,
>   the clouds thundered forth,
>   yea, your lightning bolts shot to and fro.
> [18]The crash of your thunder was in the whirlwind,
>   your lightnings lit up the world,
>   the earth quaked and trembled.
> [19]In the sea was your way,
>   your path through the mighty waters,
>   your tracks could not be seen.
> [20]You led your people like a flock,
>   by the hand of Moses and Aaron.   *(Ps. 77:16–20)*

The Psalm shares the vocabulary and concepts of neighboring cul-
tures but emphasizes the ease of divine victory. The cosmic waters
are convulsed (the waters are endowed with will) by the mere sight
of the divine warrior and his armory of storm clouds, thunder and
lightning. The power of the sea is broken by making a path through
it. Note that the Psalm ends with the installation of Moses and Aaron as leaders of the people. As will be seen below, an ordered human
society arises out of the creation process; Israel is formed as a society
when its leaders are installed.

Breaking the power of the desert by making a way through it is
shown in Deut 32:7–14, a recital of the emergence of Israel already
discussed in Chapter Two. Yahweh as an eagle makes a way through
the desert by flying with Israel, his nestling, secure on his wings: "He
came upon him in the land of wilderness . . . he spread out his wings
and took him up . . . he brought him to the high places of the earth."
In Ps 78:52–55 Yahweh leads his people through the desert to his
shrine, the holy land.

It was Second Isaiah who brought to most memorable expression the conquest of sea and desert through the making of a way

through them. Isa 40:3–5 is simply the most famous example; it is by no means the only one nor even the clearest.

> ³In the wilderness clear the way for Yahweh.
> Make straight in the desert the highway for our God.
> ⁴Every valley is to be raised up,
> every mountain and hill is to be leveled.
> The broken terrain is to become flatland,
> the steep places, a plain.⁴
> ⁵The glory of Yahweh will be revealed;
> all flesh will see it together.⁵
> The mouth of Yahweh has spoken.

A text cited twice before, 43:16–21, shows more clearly than the above text the conquest of desert by a highway, and the prophet's interpretation of the old Exodus-Conquest as a way through sea to be contrasted with the new Exodus-Conquest as a way through desert.

An important consequence follows from the ancient Near Eastern habit of conceptualizing cosmogony as a conflict of wills. The account of such a cosmogony has to be a narrative, the story of the encounter between two personal beings. The chief Mesopotamian cosmogonies, *Enuma elish* and *Atrahasis,* the Ugaritic Baal cycle, and various biblical accounts are all stories. Each has an introduction of characters, complication engendering suspense, denouement and resolution. Because the process of cosmogony was imagined as a conflict of wills, it was dramatic by its nature and hence had to be told as a story. Moderns record the process of creation impersonally.

The second difference between East and West, ancient and modern, is the emergent from the process of creation; what world comes forth? Today we popularly imagine the act of creation issuing in a physical universe where sun and stars have been set in place and where the planets have cooled down. We do not generally regard liv-

---

4. The desert referred to is of course not the sandy wastes of the Sahara but areas like those to the south and west of Judah, impassable to pack animals and humans because of precipitous ascents and descents.

5. The supremacy, or glory, of Yahweh, demonstrated in the conquest of the desert, is made visible to all in a particular place, Zion.

ing beings as part of this context. If life does come into consideration, it is usually life in its most primitive form. The study of early animals and of man is generally assigned to other branches of learning than those which deal with "creation." Human culture is not thought to be the product of creation.

In the ancient Near East, on the other hand, the emergent was a *peopled* universe. Isa 42:5 puts it nicely.

> Thus says the God Yahweh,
> (who) creates the heavens and stretches them out,
>   who spreads out the earth and what it brings forth;
> (who) gives breath to the people upon it,
>   spirit to those who walk upon it.

In Gen 1:1–2:3 the man and woman are created on the sixth day: the world has been day by day made fit for humanity. Man and woman in Gen 1:26–30 represent human society formed by God in its basic tasks and orientation. With the appearance of the man and the woman the cosmogony is complete. The society that comes forth from the cosmogonic process is organized with kingship (a frequent topic in such accounts), sexuality and marriage (cf. Gen 2:4–3:24), culture and language. It is perhaps more accurate to speak of the entire Genesis 1–11, not just the two creation accounts in Genesis 1–3, as a single cosmogony. The sequence of creation-flood-creation is paralleled in *Atrahasis,* an account of second millennium Mesopotamia. Gen 4:7–26 is a seven member genealogy that speaks of culture heroes who introduced animal husbandry, music, and metalworking, all of which are elements of human society.

That the ancient Near Eastern cosmogony typically ended with an articulated community is extraordinarily important for the Bible. Israel saw itself as the emergent of a cosmogony. It understood its national story, the Exodus-Conquest, as a cosmogony. Its essentials were given in that process. Moses and Aaron were installed according to the cosmogony in Psalm 77:16–20. Psalm 89 speaks of the installation of the Davidic kingship in its cosmogony. Most important, the land on which Israel stood before its God was given in the cosmogony. The land is the term of the story both in the historic type and in the cosmogonic type. Peoplehood was imagined concretely. Israel saw itself as complete when it was in Yahweh's land, when it had its leader and customary law.

The account of the origins of Israel, both in the historic and cosmogonic ideal types, is dramatic, a story of the conflict of wills. In versions of the historic type, Pharaoh and his armies keep the Hebrews in slavery and refuse to let them leave Egypt. Yahweh defeats Pharaoh and leads his people through the Red Sea to the land of Canaan. In versions of the cosmogonic type, the people are trapped in sea or desert, or sea/desert interposes itself between the people and God's land. Yahweh defeats the hostile force, often by making a road through it, and the people are led to safety in his precincts.

A third difference between ancient and modern accounts of creation is that modern accounts seldom explain one feature of the created world without adverting to the rest of the creation. The reason perhaps is the influence of scientific method upon popular thinking. In science a hypothesis cannot stand unless it explains all the data. If the explanation for the origin of one element in creation is self-contradictory when applied to another, the whole hypothesis falls to the ground. Hence scientific explanations, professional or popular, must be total in some sense.

Ancient explanations, on the contrary, are typically partial; they often explain just one or two segments of human society, or society from a single aspect. Other themes may appear but only one is followed through with consistency.

A fourth difference is that the old accounts were written in an age far less conscious than our own of historical development. We are acutely conscious that all living things develop; they increase or decline. Humans evolved from lower forms of life. Millions of years were required to reach the present level of the human race. Ancients readily imagined that a reality was perfectly there in its first creation, when it came fresh from the hand of God. To explain the origin of a thing was to explain its essence. Thus the man and the woman in the garden in the Genesis account of creation were depicted as complete. In this sense they had a representative character; they were typical.

There was an assumption that each living thing was there from the beginning.

II. SECOND ISAIAH AND CREATION

We need only note how dominant cosmogony is in Second Isaiah's thought, since we have touched on it in previous chapters. Israel witnesses (43:9–13; 44:6–9; 55:4–5) to the nations Yahweh's sole deity by its act of crossing the desert to Zion. By so acting it makes public that act by which gods in the ancient Near East were wont to prove their supreme power: the defeat of the enemy of the social world and the manifestation of kingship symbolized by the temple.[6] In contrast, the inert statues of the gods witness only the deadness of the ones they represent (40:18–20; 41:5–13; 44:6–22; 46:1–13).

The servant, depicted with royal and with Mosaic traits (cf. esp. 49:1–12), has truly understood the divine purpose of the Exile and the Restoration (50:4–11), and is now willing to take the risk of returning to Zion. When Zion is rebuilt and Israel (even a part of it) gathers in the sacred land, Israel lives; the nations see the glory of Yahweh in Zion.

The first and last things, Babylon and Zion, are likewise expressions of the cosmogony. First and last things can mean the repetition of the first cosmogony,[7] the Exodus-Conquest, in which Israel

---

6. Ancient literature often expresses the abstract idea of kingship over gods and humans concretely and institutionally by describing a victory in battle and the building of a temple, or the victory celebration in the palace. Often kingship is alluded to, rather than described in detail. A part, e.g. the procession of the victorious warriors to the palace or the banquet, stands for the whole, the complete idea of kingship.

7. Does Second Isaiah refer to "first creation," i.e. to the creation of the material world and the people on it before Israel came into existence? Carroll Stuhlmueller, *Creative Redemption in Deutero-Isaiah* (Analecta Biblica 43; Rome: Biblical Institute, 1970), poses the question and finds the prophet does allude to first creation though not frequently. See his Chapter 6. The question, in our opinion, is not carefully posed. The prophet speaks only of the creation, or cosmogony, in which Israel comes forth as Yahweh's people standing in his land. We do not know if he accepted the Priestly arrangement of Genesis 1–11, which does indeed speak of the creation of the world and its inhabitants *before* Israel came into being. For him, creation is the divine act of victory from which Israel emerged as a people.

emerged as a people. Babylon-Zion is the contemporary rendition of
Egypt-Canaan in the first event.[8]

---

8. The prophet's persistent use of cosmogonic language should make his commentators less ready to accuse him of being mistaken in his optimistic portrayal of life in restored Zion. The return was full of disappointments and frustrations, as Isa 56–66 attest. R. N. Whybray concludes "that in his basic prediction he was to a very large extent mistaken. Although Cyrus did capture Babylon and release the Jewish captives, and although they did return to their homes in Palestine and rebuild their national life and institutions there, Deutero-Isaiah's predictions of a future of unalloyed happiness and political power remained entirely unfulfilled." See his *Isaiah 40–66* (The New Century Bible Commentary; Grand Rapids: Eerdmans, 1975), 37–38. But one must remember his either/or conception of cosmogony—*either* primordial darkness, the dominance of desert to obstruct human society, the false honor given to the dead gods of Babylon *or* the light shining to the nations, the taming of the desert through a pathway, the recognition of the glory of the only powerful deity. For Second Isaiah the re-creation of Israel has just this significance. It is likely that his hearers would have heard his language within the frame of reference that he chose. One may question further whether the prophet is really promising a trouble-free existence to the returnees. What is important for him is that Israel continue to exist. Now that Yahweh had decided to console Israel, it could only exist in Zion.

PART TWO

Translation and Commentary of Isaiah 40–55

.

1st Speech

YAHWEH SPEAKS GOOD NEWS TO ISRAEL

[40:1–11]

[1]"Comfort, comfort my people," says your God.
[2]   "Speak consolingly to Jerusalem.
Declare to her,
    that her time of servitude is completed,
    that her sin is expiated,[1]
that she has received from Yahweh
    double for all her sins."

[3]A voice declares,
"In the wilderness clear
    the way of Yahweh.
Make straight in the desert
    the highway for our God.[2]
[4]Every valley is to be raised up,
    every mountain and hill is to be leveled.

---

1. V. 2 reflects the common view that sins of themselves bring evil effects which must be endured. Jeremiah taught that Israel must endure exile for seventy years, 25:11, 27:7 and 29:10. Second Isaiah also regards the Exile as divine punishment, but he emphasizes that it is now ended because of Yahweh's free decision to forgive.
2. These verses possibly reflect the Babylonian rite of carrying the statue of Marduk along a sacred way into Babylon on feast days. But the reference is primarily to the Israelite Exodus-Conquest and the Creation (as is made explicit 43:16–21).

The broken terrain is to become flatland,
   the steep places, a plain.
⁵The glory of Yahweh will be revealed;
   all flesh will see it together.
The mouth of Yahweh has spoken."

⁶A voice says, "Declare!"
And I said, "What shall I declare?"
"All flesh is grass,
   all its constancy like the flower of the field.
⁷The grass is withered, the flower is dead,
   for the wind of Yahweh has blown upon it.
Surely the grass is the people!
⁸The grass is withered, the flower is dead,
   but the word of our God stands forever."

⁹"Go up to a high mountain,
   O Zion, messenger of good tidings.
Raise your voice aloud,
   Jerusalem, messenger of good tidings.
Raise your voice, do not be afraid,
   say to the cities of Judah:
   'Here is your God!'
¹⁰Here is my Lord Yahweh,
   in strength he comes, his arm rules.
Here is his reward with him,
   his recompense is by him.
¹¹Like a shepherd he pastures his flock,
   in his arms he gathers the lambs.
He gathers them in his bosom,
   the mother sheep he leads."

COMMENTARY

    The opening command is abrupt and the dialogue confusing
only to readers unfamiliar with the genre—a heavenly council scene;
it is common in ancient Near Eastern literature. Similar scenes are
found in 1 Kgs 22:19–23, Isaiah 6, Job 1:6–12 and 2:1–6 and, vesti-

gially, in Gen 1:26, 11:7, Ezek 1:4–3:11 and Daniel 7. In 1 Kgs 22:19–23 and Isaiah 6, the prophet reports a heavenly declaration that determines events on earth.

The religious texts of Israel's polytheistic neighbors picture the assembly of the gods engaged in lively debate, the major deities expressing their opinions on the problem at hand. The resultant decree is oftentimes an uneasy compromise between factions among the gods. At times it is even extorted from an assembly threatened and bullied by a violent minority. In short, the divine assembly ran like most human assemblies of that time.[3]

The Bible does not hesitate to preserve the traditional picture of the assembly but changes the role of the high god; Yahweh presides masterfully over a shadowy and thoroughly subordinate court. In Isaiah 6 the "gods" now sing "holy, holy, holy," to Yahweh; they have been reduced to a choir. In Isa 40:1–8, members of the court are similarly subservient, transmitting his command with unquestioning reverence. In both texts of Second Isaiah referring to the divine assembly, chapters 6 and 40, the prophet describes himself as participating in the heavenly proceedings without giving an explanation of how he got there. Somehow he represents the people before the heavenly court, venting their sufferings in the traditional phrases of the lament psalms: "Woe is me . . . in the midst of a people of unclean lips do I dwell" (Isa 6:5 and cf. Ps 12:1–4); "How long, O Lord?" (Isa 6:11 and cf. Ps 74:10); "All flesh is grass . . . the grass is withered . . . for the wind of Yahweh has blown upon it" (Isa 40:6–8 and cf. Ps 90:5–6). Both chapters 6 and 40 portray Yahweh presiding over his royal court and issuing a decree decisive for Israel, but the two decisions are entirely different. In Isaiah 6, destruction is decreed for Israel; in Isaiah 40, forgiveness and return. It is our prophet's happy task to bring that message to his people.

The prophet reports the divine decree resulting, not from assembly discussion, but as a spontaneous word of God decreeing that "my people" is to be told gently that its sin is forgiven (vv. 1–2). Without discussion or question, officials in the court begin to implement the proclamation with specific commands, vv. 3–5.[4] One of the heavenly

---

3. See the important article of F.M. Cross, "The Council of Yahweh in Second Isaiah," *JNES* 12 (1953) 274–77.

4. Heb. *qārā'*, "to call, declare," in v. 2 is echoed in vv. 3 and 6ab.

courtiers addresses the prophet in v. 6; he is told to declare what he has heard to people on earth. Point for point in vv. 9–11 he makes known to Zion what he has seen and heard. He was told to declare (v. 6); Zion is to lift up her voice (v. 9). He saw a highway prepared for Yahweh (vv. 3–4); Zion is to announce that God is coming along it (v. 10). He saw the glory of Yahweh appearing on the road (v. 5); in Zion royal glory will surround Yahweh as he leads home his loyal subjects (v. 11).

The embodiment of heavenly act through human agency, instanced by the prophet's point for point copying of the heavenly decree, is an important principle in Second Isaiah. Yahweh's mighty wind in the unfavorable past has seared his people in 40:7: "the grass is withered, the flower is dead, for the wind of Yahweh has blown upon ($n\check{s}b$) it." In the past, Nebuchadnezzar was the agent of Yahweh's wrath. In the favorable present, the wind of the storm god becomes embodied in Cyrus the Persian king, in 41:2c–3: "(Who) has made [nations/kings] like dust with his sword, like driven chaff with his bow? He chases them, he roars on safely, by road on foot he does not march."[5] The same storm wind assists Israel in leveling the mountains that stand in its path: "You are to thresh mountains and reduce them to powder, hills you make like chaff. You will toss them in the air, the wind will carry them off, the storm will scatter them" (41:15–16) Another example of the principle is Cyrus' mimicking Yahweh shaping the world like the potter through Cyrus' mastery over kings in 41:25, "He has trampled rulers like clay, like a potter treading clay." Such examples show that reflection of the heavenly world in human institutions like temples and images, so common in the ancient Near East, tends in Second Isaiah to be transposed to correspondence between divine deeds and human actions.

We now turn to the particular way our verses shape the conventions of the heavenly council scene. The voice of God has ordered his heavenly court to console Israel (vv. 1–2). A heavenly official instantly translates that general command into concrete terms: a way is

---

5. In 40:23–24, the same storm wind of Yahweh uproots kings not appointed by him: "Scarcely are they planted, scarcely sown . . . when he blows upon them ($n\check{s}p$) they wither. . . ." The Hebrew verb $n\bar{a}\check{s}ap$ in 40:24 is related in sound and sense to $n\bar{a}\check{s}ab$ in 40:7. The wind of Yahweh is one of the ways he carries out his will on earth.

to be prepared in the desert so that the glory of Yahweh may be seen by the whole world, vv. 3–4. As elsewhere in Second Isaiah, the desert is a waterless place of sterility where no human life is possible until its death-dealing nature is altered. Yahweh's conquest is generally portrayed as removing its anti-human power; he puts water in it or makes a road through it (41:17–20; 42:15–16). To make the hostile desert fit for humans, all the features that make travel through it impossible—valleys, mountains and hills, steep and rough places—have to be eliminated.[6] The waste, once trackless, is now man's. The mastery of the very seat of sterility reveals to all the earth the heavenly supremacy, or glory, of Yahweh (v. 5). The use of creation language and language of the old Exodus-Conquest to describe the same event could not be clearer than in this passage.

It is not enough that the decision be proclaimed in heaven; it must also be proclaimed on earth. First Isaiah in his vision heard the Lord say "Whom shall I send? Who will go for us?" (6:8). This new message must likewise be communicated, and so he is told "Declare!" Before learning the wording of the passage (ancient messengers did not improvise but repeated verbatim), he must lament for his people, just as First Isaiah did in chapter 6. The prophet hears his own lament turned into a word of divine assurance in his colloquy with the heavenly being (vv. 6–8). The prophet learns the word of God is more powerful than the people's desolation.

That vv. 6–8 continue the heavenly dialogue of the previous verses has been missed by some commentators who seek to emend the two similar verses, vv. 6–8. To the command of v. 6a, "Declare!" the prophet's response, "What shall I declare?" is followed by a description of human fragility conventional in laments: "man's days are like grass quickly killed by the withering wind" (cf. Pss 90:5–6 and 103:15–16). The prophet must express honestly the exhaustion of his people whose life has been withered by Yahweh's fierce wind, "the blast of his nostrils" (Exod 15:8 and cf. Ps 48:7 and Hos 13:15). Lest there be any doubt that the prophet is representing his people and not just himself, he declares that the grass is the actual state of the people, "Surely the grass is the people." The heavenly official's

---

6. The desert is not sand dunes. Like many Middle Eastern deserts, it is a place of mountains and deep valleys.

answer to the prophet's honest reluctance is to agree with him that the people are indeed devastated at the present time; he repeats the prophet's words in v. 8a, "The grass is withered, the flower is dead." But instead of repeating the last phrase of the prophet's lament, "for the wind of Yahweh has blown upon it," he tells of God's word which can make dry bones live: "but the word of our God stands forever." That word has already set the heavenly courtiers to work; it surely will move the earth into action.

The series of proclamations initiated by God's word in v. 1 continues in vv. 9–11. The heavenly courtier has commissioned the prophet who now in his turn commissions Zion (the term Second Isaiah favors for Jerusalem) to announce to the cities of Judah, "Here is your God!" Zion is preeminently the place of divine disclosure, "From Zion shall go forth the teaching, the word of Yahweh from Jerusalem" (Isa 2:3, among other texts). Yahweh is returning to Zion in a new Exodus-Conquest, his people following his gentle yet powerful leadership (cf. Exod 15:13–18 and Ps 78:52–55). He rewards Zion for her painful separation from her children, an allusion to Jer 31:16, part of an old poem on a similar theme. The call to Zion to "go up" is meant to contrast with the command to Babylon to "go down" from her throne in 47:1, Dame Babylon being the antithesis of Dame Zion in Second Isaiah.

The opening scene is a drama. Yahweh speaks peace, his heavenly messengers act, his earthly messenger is appointed, Zion is made the place where the good news of the new divine nearness will be proclaimed. The prophet is to show his people how they are to respond; this will be his task in the discourses that follow.

2nd Speech

STRENGTH FOR AN EXHAUSTED PEOPLE

[40:12–31]

¹²Who measured in his hand the (cosmic) waters,
    took the measure of the heavens with a span,
    placed the dust of the earth in a scale?
Who weighed in a balance the mountains,
    the hills in a scale?
¹³Who took the measure[1] of the spirit of Yahweh,
    as his counselor advised him?
¹⁴Whom has he consulted for information,
    who has taught him about the path of justice,
has conveyed knowledge to him,
    has shown him the way of wisdom?
¹⁵See, the nations are a drop in the pan (of the scales),
    like clouds on the scales are they reckoned,
    see, the coastlands lift it [the pan] like dust.[2]
¹⁶Lebanon does not suffice for fuel,
    its animals do not suffice for sacrifice.
¹⁷All the nations are nothing before him,
    less than nothing and chaos are they reckoned by him.

---

1. In Prov 16:2, Yahweh takes the measure of the spirit of the man [*tōkēn* in G form] whose ways are pure in his own eyes. There seems to be a deliberate contrast here between Yahweh measuring the heavens and someone attempting to measure Yahweh's spirit (lit. wind).
2. The coastlands have no more ability to lift the pan with the weight than does dust.

¹⁸To whom will you compare God,
what form will you contrive for him?
¹⁹A statue? A craftsman casts it,
a smith plates it with gold,
trimmings of silver he smelts.
²⁰Precious wood that is set apart,
he chooses a wood that will not rot.³
He seeks a skilled woodworker
to make a statue that will not totter.
²¹Do you not know, have you not heard,
has it not been told to you from the beginning,
have you not understood how the earth was founded?
²²The one enthroned above the vault of the earth—
its inhabitants look like grasshoppers!⁴
The one stretching out like fabric the heavens,
he stretches it out like a tent to dwell in!
²³The one making princes into nothing,
rulers of the earth he has made like chaos!
²⁴Scarcely are they planted, scarcely sown,
scarcely is their stock rooted in the soil,
when he blows upon them and they wither,
the storm wind picks them up like chaff.

²⁵"To whom will you compare me,
(whom) do I resemble?" says the Holy One.
²⁶"Raise your eyes to the heavens and see.
'Who created them?' "
The one who leads their (heaven's) army in ordered ranks;
he calls them all by name!
Because of the greatness of power [rōb 'ōnîm] and the force
of might ['ammîṣ kōaḥ],
not a single one misses muster.

---

3. The last part of v. 19 and the first part of v. 20 are extremely difficult. The translation is conjectural.

4. There is a double word play here, "the one enthroned," yōšēb and "its inhabitants," yōšēbeyhā; "vault," ḥûg, and "grasshoppers," ḥûg/ḥăgābīm.

[27]Why does Jacob say,
  does Israel state,
"My situation is hid from Yahweh,
  my case escapes the notice of my God"?
[28]Do you not know, have you not heard?
An everlasting God is Yahweh,
  creator of the ends of the earth.
He does not grow faint, he does not grow weary,
  there is no searching out his wisdom,
[29]giving strength [kōaḥ] to the faint,
  for the one without power ['ônîm] he increases strength
  ['oṣmâ yarbeh].
[30]Youths may faint and grow weary,
  young men may stumble,
[31]but those who wait for Yahweh will renew their strength
  [kōaḥ],
  they will grow wings like eagles.
They will run and not become faint,
  walk and not grow weary.

COMMENTARY

According to the previous section, Zion is the goal of the march homeward. The prophet now turns his attention to those at the other end of the road—the exiles in Babylon. These he must persuade that their national God, Yahweh, is aware of their exhaustion from captivity, v. 27, and is able to strengthen them. The discourse is divided into three sections of progressively increasing length, each introduced by a question: I, vv. 12–17 (18 cola); II, vv. 18–24 (22 cola); III, vv. 25–31 (26 cola). The series of rhetorical questions about who created the world resembles the questions that Yahweh asks Job out of the whirlwind in Job 38–41, typified by the first, "Where were you when I laid the foundation of the world? Tell me if you have understanding" (38:1). The long Joban series sweeps Job from his confident position to a new openness to God's ways: "I had heard of thee by the hearing of the ear, but now my eye sees thee; therefore I despise myself, and repent in dust and ashes" (42:5–6, *RSV*). The prophet similarly intends by his questions to move his fellow exiles from stubborn passivity to openhearted readiness for action.

As seemingly random as the prophet's questions initially appear, they are arranged according to a rigorous logic. The first question, v. 12, asks who could have measured out with his own hands the traditional raw material of the world—cosmic waters, heavens, earth, along with mountains and hills, the cosmic pair often found in creation lists.[5] Who then with consummate wisdom arranged these materials into a beautiful universe (vv. 13–14)? The answer to the first series of five questions in v. 12 is "Yahweh alone"; to the second series in vv. 13–14, "no heavenly being but Yahweh." Ancient Near Eastern religion commonly held the work of creation to be the work of the assembly of the gods, or at least of several gods known for their wisdom. That possibility is excluded. Yahweh created alone.

Yahweh's mastery over the elements is expressed by his effortless weighing of them on a scale, v. 12, a metaphor to which vv. 15–16 correspond exactly.[6]

The Weighing of the World (v. 12)	The Weighing of Nations (vv. 15–16)
waters	drop of water
heavens	cloud of heaven
earth	dust of earth
mountains	Lebanon
hills	

The exiles assume that Fate now favors the Babylonians who defeated and now rule them, and the other nations who moved in to occupy the land of Judah. Second Isaiah declares that all nations are only a tiny fraction of the raw material of the world, utterly mallea-

---

5. As in Pss 114:4, 6 and 148:9; Jer 4:24; Mic 6:1; Hab 3:6; Ps 89:12, correcting MT *yāmin* to Mount Amanus. On Psalm 89, see M. Dahood, *Psalms II* (Anchor Bible 17; Garden City; Doubleday, 1968), 314.

6. For pointing out to me the balance of v. 12 with vv. 15-16, and for other comments on this speech, I am indebted to Professor Paul Mosca.

ble in the hands of Yahweh, Israel's God. The prophet makes use of language familiar to Israel from hymnody, especially the present participle commonly used for divine activity, to affirm that Israel has no one to fear now that Yahweh has forgiven them.

To understand the force of the second series of rhetorical questins in vv. 18–24, one must realize that in the East the God who created the world by arranging its elements would be expected to continue dominating those elements in a way visible to human beings. Thus in Psalm 89 Yahweh who tamed the sea and fashioned heaven and earth, Zaphon and Amanus[7] (vv. 9–12), shares that power over creation point by point with the Davidic king. It is the king who will make the domination visible to the other kings of the world: "I will place his hand on the sea, / on the Rivers his right hand. . . . Yes, I make him my firstborn, / the highest of the kings of the earth" (vv. 25, 27). The king bodies forth the power of his patron deity to the world. Thus he "presents again" that original divine domination. This "re-presentative" character of the king makes him a living image of the deity. The king then functioned like a cultic image; he is a mode of the patron god's presence. This parity in function of king and statues is assumed in our passage.

Isa 40:18 really asks what "re-presentation" of God's power over creation can the people make so as to come into contact with that power. Statues are immediately rejected because they "re-present" only human ingenuity and industry (vv. 19–20). But the most effective refutation of statues as adequate images is Yahweh himself acting visibly in the world from its beginning. Yahweh's creative activity is often expressed in the hymns of the Psalter by present participles such as we find here, *hayyōšēb*, "the one who sits enthroned," v. 22a. He has proved himself king by forcing the raw material of the world into the shape he desires; nothing of that original chaotic material[8] can represent him. Neither can the rulers of the nations. In the palace language of Phoenicia and Israel, kings were sometimes called "scions," "shoots," "plantings," perhaps to suggest that the dynasty

---

7. Dahood, *Psalms II,* 314.

8. In v. 23 *'ayin,* "nothingness," and *tōhû,* "chaos," are used, as they are in v. 17. The words describe pre-creation formlessness.

from which they sprang was eternal.[9] In vv. 23–24 the same figure is used to show the inadequacy of kings to reflect the reality of heavenly patrons. The wind of Yahweh which had once blown against Israel (40:7) blows now against those kings, to root them up. The verses have an entirely negative function: to show that the traditional images of deity, such as statues and human kings, cannot mediate Yahweh's presence.

Beside statues and kings, the only other possible equal to a god in the ancient Near East would be one of the deities in the heavenly court. This is the import of the last question: "(Whom) do I resemble?' says the Holy One" (v. 25). The questioner is told to lift his eyes to the heavens, to the Creator of all the hosts there (v. 26). As in v. 22a, the speaker designates Yahweh by the hymnic participle, here "the one who leads out heaven's army." He is undisputed general of the heavenly army (represented by the stars); the members line up unquestioningly through respect for his power, v. 26.

If then there is no powerful deity besides Yahweh, why does Israel accuse him of being in eclipse, unable to protect his client people (v. 27)? Again one finds the rhetorical pointing to Yahweh, "an everlasting God is Yahweh, / creator of the ends of the earth" (v. 28ab), like the pointing in vv. 22a and 26c. Yahweh does not wane with the change of seasons or according to locale; he is mysteriously universal (v. 28).

The second section and part of the third had the negative aim of denying to images and to kings their customary value as mediating divine presence, and of devaluing all gods but Yahweh. The last lines of part three are wonderfully positive; they show how Israel is to gain strength from Yahweh. In v. 26 the great strength of Yahweh (in Hebrew, *rōb 'ōnîm, 'ammîṣ kōaḥ*) forces the heavenly host into

---

9. The best biblical example is Isa 11:1: "There shall come forth a shoot from the stump of Jesse, and a branch shall grow out of his roots" (*RSV*). See also Dan 1:7. On the self-renewing of the stock, see Job 14:7–12. For Phoenician, see the Ahiram sarcophagus, *thtsp ḥtr mšpth*, "let his judicial scepter be broken." The word *ḥtr* in the meaning of "shoot" occurs in Isa 11:1; there may be a play on "shoot" or "offspring" in the Ahiram inscription. See further H. Donner–W. Röllig, *Kanaanäische und aramäische Inscriften* (Wiesbaden: Harrassowitz, 1962) II.4. In the Azitawwad inscription, one finds *wp'l 'nk lšrš 'dny n'm*, "I acted kindly toward the root of my sovereignty," possibly a reference to the seed royal.

submission. That same strength is now available to Israel in vv. 29–31, or rather to those in Israel who "wait for Yahweh." Waiting for Yahweh is the opposite of the attitude of v. 27, "My situation is hid from Yahweh." That their new-found strength is expressed in walking and even in running without fatigue is highly significant; they are soon to march in the procession to Zion.

3rd Speech

JUDGMENT IN FAVOR OF ISRAEL

[41:1–42:9]

¹Be silent before me, coastlands,
   let the nations wait for my decision.[1]
Let them approach to state their case,
   let us come forward together for judgment.
²Who roused from the east the graciously chosen one,[2]
   summoned him to his service?[3]
Who delivers nations into his hands,[4]
   treads upon kings?
He makes (them) like dust with his sword,
   like driven chaff with his bow.
³He chases them, he blows on unscathed,
   by road on foot he does not go.[5]

---

1. A well-known textual difficulty. MT *yaḥălîpû,* "(Let the coastlands) renew (their strength)," does not lack defenders (Rignell, de Boer, Muilenburg), but it seems to be a dittography of 40:31a. We suggest that 42:4, *ûltôrātô 'iyyîm yĕyaḥêlû,* "the coastlands wait for his teaching," forms an *inclusio,* or reprise, of 41:1, so that one should read the latter verse something like *lĕtôrātî* (or *lĕtôkahtî*) *yĕyaḥēlû,* "let the nations wait for my decision."

2. The Hebrew word *ṣedeq* is difficult to translate. Because the context is the choosing of Cyrus (see the next note), we bring out the note of legitimacy and grace in the choosing. See also 41:10, "Yes, I uphold with my gracious right hand."

3. Lit. "He summons him to his feet." Hab 3:5 speaks of Pestilence and Plague in the retinue of Yahweh the warrior, *wĕyēṣē' rešep lĕraglāyw,* "Plague went forth at his feet."

4. We take *lĕpānāyw* as the equivalent of *bĕyādāyw,* "into his hands"; it is holy war vocabulary.

5. V. 3 needs no emendation. The subject is Cyrus embodying the storm wind of Yahweh. In Isa 17:13, Yahweh beats back his enemies like dust before the storm; see

⁴Who has acted, has done this?
    The one summoning the generations from the beginning!
I, Yahweh, the first,
    with the last, I am he.

⁵The coastlands have seen and are in fear (*yr'*),
    the ends of the earth (*qěṣôt hā'āreṣ*) tremble.
They draw near and they come,
⁶each one helps (*'zr*) his neighbor,
    says (*'mr*) to his fellow, "Courage!" (*ḥzq*)
⁷The woodworker encourages (*ḥzq*) the smith,
    the one who flattens with the hammer,
    encourages (*ḥzq*) him who pounds the anvil.
He says (*'mr*) of the (gold) leaf,⁶ "It is beautiful!"
    He fixes (*ḥzq*) it with nails so it cannot move.

⁸But you, Israel, are my servant,
    Jacob whom I have chosen,
    offspring of Abraham my friend.
⁹You are the one whom I have taken (*ḥzq*) from the ends of
    the earth (*qěṣôt hā'āreṣ*),
    whom I called from its far corners.
I say (*'mr*) to you, "You are my servant,
    I have chosen you, I have not rejected you.
¹⁰Do not fear (*yr'*) for I am with you,
    do not be afraid for I am your God.
I strengthen you, I help (*'zr*) you,
    I uphold you with my victorious right hand.
¹¹They will be confused and shamed
    who rage against you.
They will be reduced to nothing and will perish
    who dispute with you.

---

also Job 13:25. In Ps 103:15–16 the wind blows (*'br*) over man, destroying him like
grass. For the verb "go" (*bô'*) used of wind, see Job 1:19.

    6. The word *debeq*, a rare noun from the verb *dābaq*, "to cling, cleave, keep
close," occurs (in the plural) in only one other place, and that obscure. It is traditionally translated "soldering, riveting" but in the light of the context of statue making, we
suggest that it refers to a bronze statue over which silver or gold leaf is laid.

¹²Search for them, you will not find them,
  those who strive against you.
They will be reduced to nothing and non-existence
  who make war against you.
¹³For I am Yahweh your God,
  who holds (ḥzq) your right hand;
  who says ('mr) to you, "Do not fear (yr'),
  I help ('zr) you."

¹⁴Do not fear, worm Jacob,
  maggot⁷ Israel.
I offer you help—oracle of Yahweh—
  your Redeemer, the Holy One of Israel.
¹⁵I have made you now into a threshing sledge,
  keen, new, sharp edged.
You are to thresh mountains, reduce them to powder,
  hills you are to make like chaff.
¹⁶You will winnow them, the wind will carry them off,
  the stormwind will scatter them.
You will rejoice in Yahweh,
  exult in the Holy One of Israel.

¹⁷The poor and needy are seeking water; there is none.
  Their tongue is dry with thirst.
I, Yahweh, will answer them;
  as God of Israel I will not abandon them.
¹⁸I will open rivers on the bare heights,
  springs in the midst of the valleys.
I will make the desert into ponds,
  the parched land into springs of water.
¹⁹I will plant cedars in the desert,
  acacias, myrtles, and olives.
I will set cypresses in the desert,
  box trees along with pines;
²⁰that people may see and acknowledge,
  observe and understand,

---

7. We accept the common comparison with Akkadian *mutu,* "maggot."

that the hand of Yahweh has done this,
the Holy One of Israel has created it. *[handwritten annotation]*

²¹Present your case, says Yahweh,
set out your evidence,
says the King of Jacob.
²²Let them draw near and let them tell us
what is about to happen.⁸
The first things—what are they?
Tell us that we may consider them,
that we may know their outcome.
Or, what is coming, inform us.
²³Tell us what is coming in the future,
that we may know you are gods.
Yes, do something—good or evil,
that we may fear and be in awe.
²⁴You are less than nothing,
your effect is non-existent,
it is an abomination to choose you.
²⁵I roused one from the north, he came;
from the rising of the sun he called (him) by name.⁹
He has trampled rulers like clay,
like a potter treading clay.
²⁶Who told this from the beginning that we might know it,
from of old that we could say, "It is true!"
No one told, no one announced,
no one heard your utterance.
²⁷The first things to Zion, here they are;
to Jerusalem I appoint a messenger.¹⁰

---

8. In vv. 22–27, the first things are the old prophecies which predicted the future actions of a god. If the god acted in accord with his predictions, it would be a proof of his or her divinity. Note the three times repeated "Tell us . . . that we may know . . ." in vv. 22, 23, and 26.

9. We adopt the reading *yiqrā' bĕšēm* for MT *yiqrā' bišmî* in accordance with 40:26. Dittography with following *wāw*. *Yôd* and *wāw* were almost indistinguishable in certain Herodian scripts. We accept the common emendation of MT *yābô'* to *yābūs* in v. 25c.

10. The verse interrupts the context and may have been inserted by a glossator who wanted to make completely clear that Zion had the first things preached to it.

[28]I looked around but there was no one,
   among them not one had advice to give,
   not one could I ask and get a response.
[29]Here are all of them—nothing;
   non-existent their deeds,
   windy chaos their images.[11]

[42:1]Here is my servant! I uphold him,
   my chosen, I am delighted with him.
 I have put my spirit[12] upon him,
   he will bring forth justice to the nations.
[2]He will not shout nor raise his voice,
   he will not cry out in the streets.
[3]The bruised reed he will not break,
   the dimly burning wick he will not snuff out.
   In truth he will bring forth justice.
[4]He shall not burn dimly, he shall not be bruised,
   when he brings justice upon the earth,
   when the coastlands wait for his teaching.
[5]Thus says the God Yahweh,
 (who) creates the heavens and stretches them out,
   (who) spreads out the earth and what it brings forth;
 (who) gives breath to the people upon it,
   spirit to those who walk upon it.
[6]I Yahweh have called you in grace,
   I have grasped your hand and protected you.
 I have made you a covenant to the peoples,
   a light to the nations;
[7]to open the eyes of the blind;
   to bring out prisoners from the dungeon,
   from the cell, those who dwell in darkness.
[8]I am Yahweh, that is my name;
   my glory I shall not give to another,
   my renown to idols.

---

11. The images are often called "nothingness," "chaos," as if they represented
only inert formlessness before the creative touch of Yahweh.
12. The spirit or wind of Yahweh that is in the striking victories of Cyrus is present in Israel in a less violent way.

⁹The first events have already taken place,
    new events I am telling;
Before they spring forth,
    I announce them.

COMMENTARY

The speech immediately preceding this one, 40:12–31, put a series of rhetorical questions to Israel designed to convince it that no power exists in the world except the power of Yahweh, and that that power is available to those who hope in him. This speech likewise exposes empty claims through relentless questions, but they are addressed to the nations, not to Israel. Moreover, the chapter progresses by means of the vivid dramatizations of a cosmic trial. The large mass of material, approximately 140 cola, is organized into a parallel structure.[13]

	A 41:1–20	B 41:21–42:9
Summons to trial	41:1, 5–7	41:21–22b
Legal questioning of nations/their gods	41:2–4	41:22c–29
Verdict on the nations and Israel	41:8–20	42:1–9

Small scale parallelism is well known as a feature of biblical poetry. The bringing into relationship of two or three lines which play off each other is the most prevalent device in the Bible; the interplay between the elements makes the poetic statement. Large scale parallelism is less widely recognized. Yet parallelism of lengthy scenes occurs, such as Ps 78:12–32//40–64,[14] Isa 49:1–13//14–26, and of characters within scenes, such as Pharaoh and Yahweh in the Priest-

---

13. The same parallel has been seen, though with modifications, by C. C. Torrey, *The Second Isaiah* (New York: Scribners, 1928), *in loc.*, W. A. M. Beuken, "The First Servant Song and Its Context," *VT* 22 (1972) and by John Goldingay, "The Arrangement of Isaiah XLI–XLV," *VT* 29 (1979) 289–99.

14. Fo ustification of parallelism in Psalm 78, see my "In Zion and David a New Beginning: An Interpretation of Psalm 78," in *Traditions in Transformation: Turning Points in Biblical Faith* (F. M. Cross volume; Ed. B. Halpern and J. Levenson: Winona Lake: Eisenbrauns, 1978) 121–41.

ly redaction of Exodus 1–15 and Dames Wisdom and Folly in Proverbs 9. The Semitic hearer presumably intuited the outline and was sensitive to its repetition. He attended to the interplay between the the two versions, an ancient instance of musical variations on a theme. The scenes, of course, are similar, not identical: the condemnation of the gods and the commission in Israel is more explicit in the second scene.

Exactly where in Israel's traditions Second Isaiah found the inspiration for the trial scene is not known. It seems too elaborate to be a transposition from the day-to-day "trial in the gate." The contrast between Yahweh and the other deities, and between Israel and the nations, is so central to the scene as to suggest that the prophet designed the scene chiefly to display those contrasts. It seems not to have arisen from a real life situation.

Each of the parallel sections, 41:1–20 and 41:21–42:9, is a complete scene. Summoned by Yahweh, the nations bring statues of their patron gods with them and repair to the place of judgment. When questioned, they are unable to produce oracles predicting Cyrus' victories, and are declared to be without power. Yahweh announces that he had predicted Cyrus' victories; hence he is the power behind them. He then addresses Israel in the most endearing terms.

There is ironic contrast between the nations chattering away to their gods who are silent (41:5–7) and Israel silent before its God who speaks abundant words of consolation (41:8–20). In addition, the word of God progressively embodies itself in earthly guises: the wind of God that was once turned against Israel because of its sins (40:7) now appears in the person of Cyrus breaking down the Babylonian Empire that holds Israel in thralldom. Vv. 2–3, generally puzzling to translators, make perfect sense if Cyrus is understood as the manifestation of the famous weapon in Yahweh, his fierce wind. Yahweh rouses Cyrus as a whirlwind. Cyrus' conquering sword has uprooted kings, a reprise of 40:23–24, making them into dry chaff which he as Yahweh's whirlwind chases about.[15] The wind in the meantime blows on (Ps 103:16), unhindered and unharmed *(šālōm)*, not constrained to follow a road like conventional armies (v. 3b). Who controls this all-conquering weapon? As in the questions of the

---

15. "Will you bully a driven leaf, chase dried chaff?" Job 13:25.

previous chapter, the answer is a present participle describing Yahweh's activity,[16] "the one who calls the generations from the first,"
i.e. the one who controls every human being and hence human history.

The action described in vv. 5–7 is actually simultaneous with
the summons and the questions of vv. 1–4 and the address to Israel
to vv. 8–16, as can be seen from comparison with the parallel in
41:21–42:9. The Bible sometimes portrays simultaneity by describing
in succession discrete scenes.

The nations draw near in fright, reassuring each other that the
silent passive images they themselves have constructed will somehow
save them from Yahweh's judgment. As can be seen from the Hebrew roots in parentheses in vv. 5–7 that are repeated in vv. 8–13, the
nations futilely address their silent gods, whereas Yahweh addresses
a silent Israel. It is a wonderfully ironic commentary upon the radi-
cally different relationship.

In his turning to Israel, Yahweh reuses some of the nations' vocabulary but in an especially affectionate way. Language of the
choosing of individuals such as Jacob, Abraham, and David (v. 9d) is
applied to the choosing of the whole people. Vv. 11–13 state that
Yahweh's choosing of Israel has given them protection from their
enemies.

Vv. 14–16 offer another illustration of the principle that Yahweh's words and actions embody themselves in human history. Yahweh addresses the people as "worm Jacob," most probably a
quotation from the lament Ps 22:6: "But I am a worm and no man."
Such laments must have been much used in the Exile. As it confesses
its weakness, Israel is shown its role in the heavenly plan. God's decree of forgiveness in 40:1 brings into being a highway; every mountain and hill is therefore to be leveled (40:4). As we have already
noted in discussing 40:12de, "mountains and hills" often occur in
lists of paired elements that are shaped into the ordered world. The
desert is at present impassable because of its sterility, i.e. no water,
and its impassable terrain, i.e. mountains and hills. Israel will be
made into a threshing sledge that will crush those mountains and
hills and make them like mounds of grain. The wind of Yahweh will

---

16. "The one enthroned . . ." in 40:21, and "the one who leads out . . ." in 40:26.

thresh and blow away this obstacle to return. Israel will rejoice to see the power of God and its own role in the salvation.

In vv. 14–16, Yahweh destroys with his weapon of wind the mountains and hills which make the way impassable. In vv. 17–20 Yahweh comes to the aid of a congregation impoverished ('ny) by the desert's aridity, answering ('ny) them by opening up rivers and planting trees there. All people, including the nations assembled with their images, will recognize that Yahweh, the God of Israel, has tamed the wilderness so that it can be traversed.

The second section, 41:21–42:9, now begins, paralleling 40:1–20 in its sequence of summons to trial, legal questioning, and verdict. The second section differs from the first in its relentless questioning. The question is whether the gods control history by their word. The nations gather and bring forward, on the divine judge's orders, their evidence. The gods must produce predictions of their actions and evidence that those predictions have been fulfilled. The only way to prove that a certain deity is behind the greatest event of the day, the military success of the Persian Cyrus, is to produce old prophecies predicting his success. But the gods are silent, their dumbness leading Yahweh to his verdict in v. 24, repeated in v. 29, which can be paraphrased; "I find you are nothing, belonging to the pre-creation chaos which exists no longer. Your influence in the world is non-existent. To honor your image makes one unholy."

After the initial verdict, Yahweh declares that it is he who has stirred up Cyrus, who now tramples kings as a potter tramples clay. Just as Cyrus in the first parallel, 41:2–3, embodied Yahweh's creative weapon of wind, so here he embodies the creative power of Yahweh "the shaper of clay" (another biblical way of expressing creation). None of the nations who have brought their images are able to say they heard their gods predict Cyrus' victories (v. 28). The verdict of v. 24 is pronounced again in v. 29—non-existence.

The same authority that pronounced the gods null and void now pronounces Israel "my servant" (42:1). As the questions to the national gods were more searching in 41:21–29 than in 41:2–3, so the commission of Israel is more explicit than in 41:8–20. The choice of Israel as Yahweh's servant is made as part of the verdict of the nullity of the nations' deities/images. Israel becomes by implication Yahweh's image, not by its static being but by its activity in carrying out the will of Yahweh. Yahweh will not entrust his heavenly glory to a stone statue: "My glory I will not impart to another, / my praise (worthiness) to idols" (42:8bc). Yet he will uphold Israel, put his spirit upon it while it makes his justice known to the world (42:1, 4).

Even more than in 41:8–10, the choice of Israel is expressed in language formerly used for the choice of prophets and kings, especially the latter, e.g. "my servant," "my chosen," "I put my spirit upon him."[17] The phrase "to bring forth justice to the nations," which occurs twice, is difficult; it may mean the divine justice the new king introduced into the land upon his accession. "And David became king over all Israel and David administered justice and righteousness to all his people."[18] We shall see other examples of formerly royal functions now exercised by the people. Here the office is exercised, but not by the proclamation that would be expected from a king nor by force. Nonetheless "divine justice and decision" will be implemented by the servant. Vv. 5–7 will show how.

Creation in Deutero-Isaiah issues in a peopled universe (v. 5b–c). Of the many peoples Yahweh has called one to a special task (v. 6). The controverted phrase descriptive of that task, "I have made you a covenant to the people, a light to the nations," most probably is adapted from old royal language designating the Davidic king as witnessing his patron God's (Yahweh's) glory on earth, among the peoples and nations.[19] The meaning of v. 6 then is the same as v. 4: Israel is to make clear to the world Yahweh's sovereignty. V. 7 specifies that message of sovereignty. The very announcement of it is a creative act, defeating the darkness of ignorance. The verse states the same truth as v. 6 in a different way, but in both vv. 6 and 7 darkness is replaced by light: blindness is overcome, prisoners (those who dwell in darkness) are let out of jail. Israel here again becomes on earth the instrument of Yahweh's creative word. V. 9 announces that the first things, the stirring up of Cyrus to defeat kings, have already occurred. The new thing, Israel's role in cooperating with Yahweh's work, is now announced ahead of time, so that Israel may cooperate with full consciousness.

---

17. Isa 11:2, "And the Spirit of Yahweh shall rest upon him . . ."

18. This interpretation is suggested by Moshe Weinfeld, *Deuteronomy and the Deuteronomic School* (Oxford: Clarendon, 1972) 152–55.

19. See further on 43:9–12; 49:6–8, and 55:4–5.

4th Speech

THE DIVINE WARRIOR REMOVES
THE OBSTACLES TO
HIS PEOPLE'S RETURN

[42:10–43:8]

[10]Sing to Yahweh a new song,
  his praise from the ends of the earth.
Let the sea roar[1] and its creatures,
  the coastlands and those who inhabit them.
[11]Let the desert and its towns raise a shout,
  the villages where Qedar dwells.
Let the inhabitants of Sela shout,
  let them sing from the top of the mountains.
[12]Let them give glory to Yahweh,
  tell his praiseworthy acts in the coastlands.
[13]Yahweh, a warrior, marches forth,
  a man of war, he rouses his anger.
He shouts, he roars aloud,
  against his enemies he shows himself mighty.
[14]For a long time I kept silent,
 I did nothing, I restrained myself.
Now I cry out like a woman in labor,
  I snort, I pant.

---

1. MT *yôrĕdê hayyām,* "those who go down to the sea," makes little sense. We
borrow from Pss 96:11 and 98:7 *yir 'am hayyām.*

[15]I will dry up mountains and hills,
    all their vegetation I will dry.[2]
I will make rivers into coastlands,[3]
    pools I will dry up.
[16]I will enable the blind to walk in a way they knew not,
    in paths they did not know I will enable them to walk.
I will make the darkness before them into light,
    the rough ways into level ground.
These are my words,
    I perform them, not omitting a one.
[17]In retreat, covered with shame,
    those who put their trust in a statue,
    those who declare to an image,
    "You are our god!"
[18]You deaf—hear!
    You blind—look and see!
[19]Who is as blind as my servant,
    as deaf as the messenger whom I send?
Who is blind as the dedicated one,
    blind as the servant of Yahweh?
[20]Though he sees many things, he does not observe.[4]
    though his ears are open, he does not hear.

---

2. Contrary to the picture conveyed by many translations, e.g. "I will lay waste mountains and hills, / and dry up all their herbage," of RSV, Yahweh does not sear the hills with a burning wind. Rather the picture is exactly that of Ps 104:6–9: "The deep covered it [earth] like a garment, over the mountains the waters stood. At your rebuke they [the waters] fled, at the sound of your thunder they rushed away. They went up the mountains, they went down the valleys, to the place which you founded for them. The boundary you set they shall not cross, they shall never again cover the earth." The translation is discussed in my "A Note on Ps 104:5–9," in *JBL* 100 (1981) 87–89. Yahweh frees the mountains and hills from the salt waters. They are the first part of the fertile earth to appear in some accounts of creation.

3. MT *'iyyîm* "coastlands" is to be retained. The picture is the same as the previous verse. Yahweh confines the waters covering the earth to their proper sphere; they stop at coastlines.

4. We have smoothed changes in person in our translation. MT may preserve ancient variants: *rā'ît* 2nd masc. sing. perf. and *tišmōr*, and *ra'ôt* inf. construct and *yišmōr*.

²¹It pleased Yahweh for his own justice's sake,[5]
    that [the servant] should glorify the Teaching and exalt it.[6]
But this was a people robbed and plundered,
    trapped in holes, all of them,
    imprisoned in dungeons.
²²They are given over to plunder, with none to rescue,
    to despoilment, with none to say "Give back!"
²³If you would only give a hearing to this,
    attend and heed for the future!
²⁴Who gave up Jacob to despoilment,
    Israel to plunderers?
Was it not Yahweh against whom we sinned,
    in whose ways they refused to walk,
    whose teaching they would not obey?[7]
²⁵He poured out upon them fury,
    his wrath and the violence of war.
It blazed all around him but he did not recognize it;
    it burned him, he did not understand.

⁴³:¹But now, thus says Yahweh,
    the one who created you, Jacob,
    the one who fashioned you, Israel.
"Do not fear, for I have redeemed you,
    I have called you by your name, you are mine.
²When you cross the waters, I will be with you,
    the rivers, they shall not overwhelm you.
When you walk through fire, you will not be burned;
    the flame shall not consume you.
³For I am Yahweh your God,
    the Holy One of Israel, your savior.

---

5. The other instance of the idiom is 53:10, "It pleased Yahweh to bruise him."

6. The "teaching" seems to refer to the consistent tradition that Israel would be punished by the loss of their land when they sinned. It may more specifically refer to the teaching that First Isaiah sealed up with his disciples when his message was meeting with disbelief, 8:16 and 30:8: a dark age of punishment was to come to be followed by an age of light.

7. The mixing of first and third person plural appears to be deliberate. No great distinction is made between the people of the past who failed to repent and the present generation who likewise fail.

I give Egypt in ransom for you,
   Ethiopia and Seba in exchange for you,
⁴because you are precious in my sight,
   honored, and I love you.
I give men in exchange for you,
   peoples instead of you.
⁵Fear not, for I am with you.
   From the east, I bring your folk,
   from the west, I gather you in.
⁶I say to the north, 'Give back!'
   to the south, 'Do not withhold!'
Bring my sons from afar,
   my daughters from the ends of the earth,
⁷all those who are called by my name!
   For my glory I have created them,
   have fashioned, have made them.
⁸Bring forth the people who are blind yet have eyes,
   the deaf yet who have ears."

COMMENTARY

One's first impression of this discourse is that it is a divine address forgiving Israel for its blindness. Comparison with certain psalms suggests however that the section is at root a song of victory; see Psalms 93, 96, 97, 98 and 99. Psalms 96 and 98 are the most relevant in determining the genre of our passage. Both begin with the same phrase; "Sing to Yahweh a new song," and both use nearly identical invitatory language, "Let the sea roar and its creatures." There are also important thematic similarities between the Psalms and Second Isaiah. The world, human and inanimate, ascribes to Yahweh alone among the heavenly beings glory appropriate to his creation victory: "For great is Yahweh . . . he is to be feared above all gods. For all the gods of the peoples are idols; but Yahweh made the heavens" (Ps 96:4–5). His creation has been effected through war: "His forearm has won him victory, his holy arm" (Ps 98:7). The entire world is to see and acknowledge his mastery: "Ascribe to Yahweh, O families of the earth, ascribe to Yahweh glory and strength" (Ps 97:7). Israel, however, has a special duty to proclaim the virtues of its own God: "Tell among the nations, 'Yahweh reigns!'" (Ps 96:10 and cf. Pss 96:3; 97:8–12; 99:1–9).

Only against the conventions of the songs of Yahweh's creation victory can this discourse be understood. The invitatory, calling upon the wide world of nature and man to acknowledge Yahweh's glory, appropriately introduces the divine warrior as he goes out to combat. In a monologue, Yahweh boasts of the destruction he will bring with his wind against chaotic waters and darkness. Yahweh boasts in typical warrior fashion that the blind, those dominated by darkness, will now be able to journey. V. 17 says that since Yahweh alone has power, those who trust in the images of other gods are bound to be shamed—a commonplace in songs to Yahweh the Creator.[8]

We have already remarked regarding the songs that Israel as Yahweh's special people has a special witnessing role: to make known to the nations what he has done or is about to do. But Israel itself is dominated by blackness, is deaf and blind; it cannot see the divine deeds or hear the divine words (42:18–20). The phrase, "It pleased Yahweh for his own justice's sake," expresses inscrutable divine purpose in the face of human frailty.[9] Yahweh affirms the servant's task of glorifying the "teaching," i.e. demonstrating on earth that the just purpose of Yahweh is triumphant. As in the "fourth servant song" (52:13–53:12) where there is a second reference to the good pleasure of Yahweh, the divine purpose is revealed as divine through human weakness. Hence v. 22 portrays vividly the weakness of the exilic community, its desperation and vulnerability. The wish is expressed that Israel would realize that its misery and blindness are due, not simply to bad luck, but to their turning from their God and his divine purpose or teaching (*tôrâ,* v. 24c). The full violence of war that has fallen upon them is the wrath of Yahweh (v. 25).

The end of the blindness that immobilizes Israel comes about as a divine decision, not as any self-initiated enlightenment. Israel can now pass through the chaotic waters (43:2) that have been controlled

---

8. Pss 96:5; 97:7; 135:15–18.
9. Isa 53:10, cited in note 4. Yahweh is pleased to affirm the servant's task of proving valid the "teaching," Yahweh's authoritative word.

by Yahweh (42:15cd); it can go through the fire (43:2cd) whose heat had so recently burned them (42:25).

Vv. 3–4 are to be taken closely together. "I am Yahweh *your* God, the Holy One *of Israel, your* savior," means that Yahweh prefers his own people to other nations (v. 4). Yahweh's favoring of his own prepares the way for the commands to bring his people from the four quarters of the world. All his sons and daughters, all those carrying his name, are to come (vv. 5–7a). He created them for his glory, that his cosmic authority might appear on earth.

The prophet has called the sons and daughters blind and deaf in 43:8.[10] In so branding them, he invites them to repent and to recognize the opportunity they have to experience with full consciousness their re-creation by Yahweh. Every act of Yahweh in the entire discourse enables the people to move, to return to Zion. Flood waters, encompassing primordial darkness, rough terrain, all fall victim to the divine warrior's attack. The once-blind people may walk and march (42:13–16). The people's present situation is the opposite of moving; they are holed up in caverns, hiding from attack (42:22). Yahweh's favor now enables them to "cross through waters," to "walk through fire" (43:2). Yahweh "causes them to come" (43:5–7). The last command is to bring the people forth (43:8). The impression given is that to move back to Zion is to take part in creation and to remain in Babylon is to yield to the domination of chaotic, anti-community forces. The prophet, eager to lead his people, puts before them the fundamental choice—to remain static or to move.

---

10. We take, with *NJV,* these verses with the preceding rather than with the following. The next section appears to be placed here by reason of the catchword principle.

5th Speech

ISRAEL RAISED TO BE A WITNESS TO YAHWEH

[43:9–44:5]

⁹Let all the nations gather together,
  let the peoples assemble.
"Who among them has announced this,
  has proclaimed the former things?¹
Let them produce their witnesses to prove them true,
  that people may hear, and say, 'It is true!'
¹⁰You are my witnesses—oracle of Yahweh—
  my servant whom I have chosen,
so that you may know and believe in me,
  that you may understand that I am he.
Before me no god was formed,
  after me none will exist.
¹¹I, I am Yahweh,
  there is no savior beside me.
¹²I announce, then I save,
  I proclaim; no alien (god) is² among you.
You are my witnesses—oracle of Yahweh—that I am God;
¹³ever since day was, I am he.

---

1. I.e. the events that have already happened.
2. "Is" in the sense of saving presence. For the sense, see Deut 32:12: "Yahweh alone led him; no strange god was with him."

No one can wrest (anything) from my hand,
   I act; who can stay it?"

¹⁴Thus says Yahweh, your Redeemer,
   the Holy One of Israel,
For your sake I send to Babylon,
   I bring down all the bars.
The glad shouts of the Chaldeans will be turned to cries of
   woe.³
¹⁵I am Yahweh, your Holy One,
   Creator of Israel, your King.

¹⁶Thus says Yahweh,
The one who makes a way in the Sea,
   a path in the Mighty Waters,
¹⁷the one who musters chariot and horse,⁴
   all the mighty army.
They lie prostrate, no more to rise,
   they are extinguished, quenched like a wick.
¹⁸Recall no more the former things,
   the ancient events bring no longer to mind.⁵
¹⁹I am now doing something new,
   now it springs forth, do you not recognize it?
I am making a way in the wilderness,
   paths⁶ in the desert.
²⁰The wild beasts will honor me,
   jackals and ostriches.
For I have placed waters in the wilderness,
   rivers in the desert,

---

3. This part of v. 14 is obscure. Analogy with 45:1–5 suggests that Cyrus is the one sent against Babylon "for your sake." Cf. the phrase "for the sake of my servant Jacob" in 45:4. No object of the verb is mentioned, perhaps in order to emphasize divine initiative. For the "bringing down" of the walls of a fortified city, see Amos 3:11 and Prov 21:22.
4. The meaning is that Yahweh is ultimate chief of the Egyptian army.
5. I.e., stop using these as your national story.
6. We read *ntybwt* for MT *něhārôt* with 1QIsaaᵃ and according to sense.

to give drink to my chosen people,
²¹the people whom I have formed for myself,
to narrate my praiseworthy deeds.

²²But you did not call me, Jacob,
you did not weary yourself (in prayer) because of me,
Israel.[7]
²³You did not bring me sheep for your whole burnt offerings,
nor honor me with your sacrifices.
I did not impose meal offerings upon you,
did not weary you with (the burden of) frankincense.
²⁴You did not purchase for me fragrant reed,
with the fat of your sacrifices you did not feed me.
But you did impose your sins upon me,
you did weary me with your iniquities.
²⁵I, I am the One,
the One who wipes away your rebellions for my sake,
who does not mark your sins.
²⁶Rehearse your story for me, let us decide together,
narrate your version, that you may be proved right.
²⁷Your first father sinned,
your spokesman rebelled against me.
²⁸I profaned the holy princes,
I delivered Jacob to destruction,
Israel to mockery.

⁴⁴:¹And now hear, Jacob my servant,
Israel whom I have chosen.
²Thus says Yahweh your maker,
the one who formed you, from birth helped you.
Do not fear, my servant Jacob,
Jeshurun whom I have chosen.
³For I will pour water on the parched soil,
streams on the dry ground.
I pour my spirit upon your descendents,
my blessing upon your offspring.

---

7. For the phrase "to weary oneself in moaning (in prayer)," see Pss 6:6 and 69:3.

[4]They shall spring forth like grass,
   like willows along water courses.[8]
[5]One will say, "I am Yahweh's";
   another will use the name "Jacob."
Another will mark his arm "Yahweh's property,"
   and adopt the name "Israel."

COMMENTARY

As the opening lines show, the speech is delivered before the assembled nations of the world. Some of its concerns are found also in a previous speech before the nations, 41:1–42:9: the god's heavenly honor and power are reflected through earthly instruments particularly through the fortunes of his people; the emphasis on theodicy; the use of legal language and questioning to establish the case for Yahweh. The first assembly was a courtroom drama in which Yahweh destroyed the nations' case in hard cross-examination, and upheld Israel. The present speech (not drama) focuses exclusively on Israel and adopts a rebuking tone for the most part. The scene of the assembly of the nations can be shaped differently for different purposes.

Unlike the earlier speech this one does not rely on the simple contrasts of drama to make its points; its dense reasoning requires extended analysis. The first part, 43:9–13, sets the scene: the nations are summoned to a trial in which they are told to witness to their god's power, Israel being singled out as Yahweh's witnesses (v. 10a). This is the first time we have met the word "witness" which will occur again later in Second Isaiah (44:8–9 and 55:4). It refers to Israel's function of revealing to the nations that its God Yahweh is unique in the pantheon. Demonstrating to the nations was a function exercised in other times by Israelite kings. Appointed by the Most High God as his regent upon earth, the king displayed his God's unique power on earth. The king confesses: "Thou didst deliver me from strife with the peoples; / thou didst make me head of the nations; / people

---

8. There is a clear analogy between the sterile desert and the sterile people; both are cured by the creative touch. The healing of both humans and nature is also strikingly narrated in Isaiah 34.

whom I had not known served me. / As soon as they heard of me
they obeyed me; / foreigners came cringing to me" (Ps 18:43-44 / / 2
Sam 22:44–45 *RSV*). Psalm 89 describes Yahweh's world-establish-
ing victory over Sea in vv. 9–13. He then shares point by point with
his Davidic king the victory just won: "I will place his hand on the
Sea, / on the Rivers his right hand. . . . Yes I make him my firstborn,
/ the highest of the kings of the earth" (vv. 25, 27). The last phrase,
"the highest (*'elyôn*) of the kings of the earth," shows that Yahweh's
royal regent plays the same role vis-à-vis the other kings as Yahweh
does vis-à-vis the other gods, at least in principle. In short the old
royal role of witnessing to the dynasty's patron god has been transferred to the people.

To what precisely does Israel witness? That question is answered in vv. 10–13, constructed of parallel sections, vv. 10–11 / /
12c–13. V. 12ab is the centerpiece which is given importance by its
position. A diagram of the verses will clarify the sense.

> A. *Appointment of Israel as witnesses:* "You are my witnesses,"
> v. 10, elaborated in v. 10bcd.
> *Its witnessing:* no God except Yahweh exists, v. 10ef.
> no God except Yahweh acts ("saves") v.
> 11ab.

> B. *Proof:* I am the only God who acts effortlessly according to
> his word, v. 12ab.

> A. *Appointment of Israel as witnesses,* "You are my witnesses,"
> v. 12c.
> *Its witnessing:* no God except Yahweh exists, vv. 12d–13a.
> no God except Yahweh acts (no other god
> can stop his work), v. 13bc.

Amid the double command to witness, v. 12ab stands out by its central position. The proof that Yahweh is God from of old is his ability
to announce beforehand what he will do, or, in other words, to shape
the world by his mere word.

The first section states the principle abstractly; the second section specifies it. After stating the principle, Second Isaiah must an-

swer an obvious objection: if Yahweh alone saves, and no power can snatch from his hand, how did Israel end up captive to Babylon? The answer is that Yahweh sent them there somehow for Israel's sake, without his ceasing to be Israel's special God. The end of the verse is corrupt and is left untranslated.

Vv. 16–21, the clearest description of the creation of Israel in Second Isaiah, is the core of the speech. Vv. 16–18 describe "the first things," "the ancient events"—the victory at the sea which brought Israel into existence. "Sea/Mighty Waters" are vanquished by the making of a path through them so that Israel may cross over. In the same way the human obstacles to Israel's movement, Pharaoh and his troops, are likewise vanquished. As impressive as that story is, an even more impressive text is to replace it as the national story. The new story is a creation victory, the vanquishing of another chaotic force equal to the "Sea//Rivers" in destructiveness—the "Wilderness//Desert." The worship of the animals of the wilderness shows how thoroughly its sterile horrors have been brought under the power of Yahweh. In the Bible animate and inanimate nature joins with man in praising the Lord. It leads us to expect that human beings in the person of Israel will soon join the public confession. Another sign of the completeness of the domination of aridity is the abundance of fresh water, enough to quench Israel's thirst. The people at last are formed in their full social structure (v. 21a), fed and able to narrate the praiseworthy deeds that brought them into existence (v. 21b).

It is precisely over the people's duty to recognize the creative hand of their God and sing his praises—in short regarding their witnessing—that the prophet rebukes his people (vv. 22–28). The rebuke of vv. 22–24 can be paraphrased. Though I have done a new creative deed, making the desert into a highway, you have not called me, i.e. proclaimed me as your God. Neither have you wearied yourself over me, i.e. in the sense of wearying yourself in mournful tears. In view of the destruction of the Temple, I did not impose upon you the sacrificial worship you were not able to give. You did not call me. You positively burdened me with sin. You have not therefore narrated my praise as my own people ought to do.

Vv. 25–28 respond to the rebuke of vv. 22–24. In words reminiscent of v. 11a, Yahweh announces forgiveness for Israel's refusal up to now to proclaim the great deeds, to proclaim that it is Yahweh's

people. Any illusion Israel might have that its recalcitrance is a simple error of the present generation, easily remedied by its own efforts,
is exposed as folly in vv. 26–28. Israel congenitally has been a sinner
and has continually invited divine punishment from its beginnings
(vv. 27–28).

Israel is appointed to witness to its God but is unable to recognize Yahweh. What is the solution to the problem? The answer is
contained in the next section, 44:1–5. Yahweh reveals himself as the
one who creates Israel. Nearly synonymous terms are used: "my servant," "the one whom I have chosen"; "the one who made you,"
"the one who forms you," "the one who has aided you from your
birth." The designations "my servant" and "my chosen," each used
twice in 44:1–2 (also at the beginning in 43:10b), were used of the
Israelite king in the monarchic period.

Divine initiative will make all the difference in Israel's ability to
take on its responsibilities. The manner of the initiative is stated in
vv. 3–5. The hand that healed the arid chaos of the desert in 43:19–
20 will heal the aridity of Israel in 44:3–4. In the opening vision the
prophet had lamented that the wind of Yahweh in punishment had
withered the flower of Israel: "The grass is withered, the flower is
dead, / for the wind of Yahweh has blown upon it. / Surely the grass
is the people" (40:7). In the next verse, the prophet was told that the
word of Yahweh will transform the withered people: "The grass is
withered, the flower is dead, / but the word of our God will exist
forever." Here the wind or spirit of Yahweh makes the people
bloom. Now the resurrected people will indeed be witnesses to the
saving power of Yahweh. They will literally carry the name of Yahweh upon their persons and proclaim to all that they are his people.
Israel then is truly the witness to Yahweh the only God.

6th Speech

WITNESSES TO THEIR MAKER

[44:6–23]

6Thus says Yahweh the King of Israel,
    its Redeemer, Yahweh of hosts.
"I am the First, I am the Last,
    apart from me there is no god.
7Who like me can announce,[1]
    can tell and so prove himself my equal?
Who announced[2] from of old events yet to happen,
    told to them what is to take place?
8Do not fear and do not be shaken!
    Have I not from of old announced and told you?[3]
You are my witnesses: Does a God exist beside me,
    a rock which I do not know?"[4]

9The makers of statues are all nothing;
    their venerated (images) cannot act;

---

1. For Second Isaiah, the proof of divinity lies in the god's ability to act without interference. This ability is demonstrated by the god's announcing ahead of time what he will do.

2. We adopt with most commentators a redivision of the consonants yielding the present translation.

3. V. 8b repeats the verbs "announce" and "tell" that have occurred already in v. 7bc.

4. We read 'im for MT 'ên, to make a double question hă ... 'im. Confusion between the letters mêm and nûn is one of the most common errors in Hebrew manuscripts.

their witnesses cannot see,
they cannot think, so they end up looking foolish.
¹⁰Who makes a god,
casts a statue
that cannot benefit?
¹¹All of its [the god's] guild members look foolish,
its craftsmen are only human beings!
They gather together, they stand up,
they fear, they are shamed.
¹²The worker in iron incises,[5]
he works over the coals.
With a hammer he shapes it,
he fashions it with a strong arm.
If he takes no food, his strength fails,
if he drinks no water, he grows weak.
¹³The worker in wood stretches out a measure,
he marks out its shape with a stylus.
He fashions it with a scraping tool,
with a compass marks out its shape.
He makes it the image of a man,
the beauty of a human to put in a temple!

¹⁴He goes out to cut a cedar,[6]
he selects an ilex and an oak.
He sets aside trees of the forest for his use,
he plants a fir; the rain makes it grow.
¹⁵It becomes something for a man to burn,
he takes it to warm himself.

---

5. The MT reads *ma'aṣad*, "axe, cutting tool." One could translate "the crafts-man in iron, with his tools," with *NJV*, or take the *mêm* as a *-mi* particle with *barzel*, and understand *'aṣad* as a verb.

6. As a tentative solution to this textual problem, I have adopted the suggestion of D. Winton Thomas, "Isaiah XLIV.9–20: A Translation and Commentary," *Hommages à André Dupont-Sommer* (ed. A. Caquot and M. Philonenko: Paris: Adrien-Maisonneuve, 1971) 326. He suggests *hlk lkrt lw* has become corrupt through haplography. Such an emendation at least has the merit of supporting a certain logic: the forester goes out to the forest, but before actually cutting he selects certain trees that are suitable and sees that they are in good locations for growing well.

Yes, he lights it and bakes bread.[7]
He also makes a god for people to worship,
 he fashions an image that they adore.
[16]Half of it he burns,
 with that half he cooks meat,
 he eats the roast and is full.[7a]
He warms himself and says, "Aah,
 I feel warm, I am near the fire!"[8]
[17]The other half he makes into a god,
 an image for him to adore and worship.
He prays to it and says,
 "Save me for you are my god!"

[18]They do not recognize, they do not understand;
 too clouded are their eyes to see,
 their minds to understand.
[19]They do not grasp,
 they lack the wit and knowledge to say,
"One half I burned,
 I baked bread on its coals,
 I roasted meat and I ate.
The other half I made into an abomination,
 a block of wood to adore."

[20][A chaser of ashes!
A deluded mind has led him astray,
 he cannot save himself,
 he does not say, "Surely it is a lie in my right hand!"][9]

[21]Remember these things, O Jacob,
 Israel, that you are my servant,

---

7. Keeping warm and baking bread around the one fire. The actions are simultaneous.
 7a. Transposition of verses for the sake of clarity.
 8. Lit. "I see (experience) the fire!"
 9. The verse appears to be a gloss. It breaks the descriptive ironic tone of the narrative.

I made you, you are my servant,
   Israel, you are not forgotten by me.
[22]I wipe your rebellions away like a mist,
   your sins like a cloud.
Return to me for I have redeemed you.
[23]Shout, O heavens, for Yahweh has acted,
   shout aloud, O depths of the earth.
Break into singing, O mountains,
   forests with all your trees!
For Yahweh has redeemed Jacob,
   he has got glory for himself in Israel.

COMMENTARY

This discourse is another instance of the prophet's fascination with the ancient idea that each nation reflects the virtue of its patron deity and maker. By now the prophet assumes that his hearers are familiar with the conventions of the scene; he concentrates on one theme without detailing the whole. Yahweh appoints Israel to witness to his unique lordship. The idiom is Deutero-Isaian; compare vv. 6–9 with 41:21–23 and 43:9–12. In dramatic contrast to Yahweh, the human "creators" of the metal and wood "witnesses" are shown exhausting themselves in the manufacture of their gods (vv. 9–19). Yahweh has formed Israel to display his glory; they have only to turn to him to wipe away the effects of their rebellion which has so far obscured their role (vv. 21–22). The invitation to nature to sing, like 49:3, celebrates the divine forgiveness and commission described in the preceding verses.

Nearly all recent commentators have denied these verses to Second Isaiah. The small handful who admit he is the author treat vv. 9–20 as separate, unconnected to vv. 6–8 and 22–23. Yet there is a single idea expressed in the passages which is genuinely Deutero-Isaianic. The double relationship "Yahweh: Israel::the gods (or their images):the nations," seen already in 41:1–42:9, appears here also. One objection to the unity of the passage is the observation that vv. 6–8 and 21–23 are poetry and vv. 9–20 are prose; hence the two sections are incompatible. The truth is rather that editors have printed vv. 6–8 and 21–23 as poetry and vv. 9–20 as prose; the recent *Biblia*

Hebraica Stuttgartensia prints the entire section as poetry. Rare
words in the section have led to textual corruption and to confusion
and repetition. Second Isaiah elsewhere uses different metrical ar-
rangements within the same poem, e.g. 41:1–13. The poet is as free
with prosody as he is with genres; he can use different modes in the
same poem.

   As free as the prophet is with the genre of national trial, its conventions still prove to be the best guide to the thought of the passage.
Yahweh identifies himself as the special God of Israel, as its king by
reason of creating it, and its redeemer by reason of leading it in the
Exodus-Conquest (v. 6ab). Creation and Exodus-Conquest are to the
prophet a single act issuing in the formation of Israel.

   Yahweh states his unique divinity in dramatic fashion. The initial statement is by way of merism, i.e. extremes which express the
totality of the spectrum: first and last (v. 6cd). There is no beginning
or end to Yahweh; he exists always. In the language of polytheism, a
god is supreme by being superior to the other gods in the pantheon.
Here that tradition of superiority-by-comparison is employed. Yahweh is the only God because only he successfully proves his divinity
by announcing beforehand what he will do. Other claimants to deity
are challenged to make known their plans beforehand so that people
may see whether deed matches prediction. Israel has heard ahead of
time the promises of its God and so are witnesses. As explained in
the previous chapter, the role of witness to the patron deity's power,
once done by the king as the divine regent, is now fulfilled by the
people. Knowing the divine words or promises (that is the meaning
of "surely I have announced them of old *to you*" in v. 8b), Israel
must now render those promises visible by its actions. Its actions as
witness are described in vv. 21–22, to turn to Yahweh as its creator
for that forgiveness of their rebellion that will enable them to be true
servants and witnesses.

   Just as Yahweh's divinity is proved in comparison with other
so-called deities, so Israel's witnessing is effected in comparison with
other so-called witnesses. Thus the great part of the speech is a series
of sketches of the activities of the witnesses of the other side. The section vv. 9–20 has several unusual words and difficult logic, confusing
interpreters from at least the time of the ancient Greek translators.
An outline and paraphrase of these verses may help. Vv. 9–11 are to

be taken closely with vv. 7–8, as the recurrence of words in both sections suggest. Israel is "my witness" (v. 8c), whereas the statues are "their witnesses" (v. 9c); Israel is not to fear *(pāhad,* v. 8a), whereas the statue makers fear *(pāhad,* v. 11d); Israel can see and know, whereas the images cannot: the statues are many whereas there is none beside Yahweh. After the depiction of both groups of witnesses in vv. 8–11, there follow several dramatizations of the nations "witnessing" to their gods/statues. The nations in the person of the craftsmen act and speak, in so doing revealing the real nature of their gods.

The first illustration is of metal workers strenuously shaping a piece of raw metal into a god. But the maker of the statue must expend all his energy in his creation—quite the opposite of the picture of Yahweh giving strength to an exhausted Israel in 40:29.[10] In the next sketch, that of carpenters making a wooden statue (v. 13), the result is only a human image—to be set incongruously in the temple of a god! The next few verses, vv. 14–15, not entirely clear, concentrate on the raw material of the statue just described in v. 13 and its incongruous uses. The work of marking out and cutting the material is entirely the work of man. As the gods had nothing to do with the selection and growth of the wood of the statues, they obviously are just as helpless regarding the use made of wood. The scene begins with the man keeping warm around the wood fire while he waits for his bread to bake. We are suddenly told that the very man who depends on the wood to keep himself warm and fed makes the statue that everyone will adore (vv. 14–15). Vv. 16–19 develop the same thought with explicit irony and with studied contrast between the unwitting activity (vv. 16–17) and its real significance (vv. 18–19). Human beings draw true sustenance (heat and cooked food) not from the finished statue but from the material before it is made into a god. Before the burning wood he exclaims artlessly (v. 16de) whereas to the god, made entirely by man, he utters a plea for help. V. 20 appears to be one of the few glosses in Second Isaiah. Its judgmental

---

10. There seems to be an allusion to 40:29 where Yahweh gives strength *(kōah)* to an exhausted *(yā'ep)* Israel. Here, in 44:12, the maker of the statue of the god may grow weak *(wayyî'āp)* and lose his strength *(kōah).*

tone, its heavy-handedness, and even its style are out of harmony with the restrained ironic narration of the rest of the passage.

The frenetic activity of the pagan idol makers makes the reader ask: what activity should Israel engage in? The answer is contained in vv. 21–22: Israel is to "remember these things," i.e. to live from the story of the unique lordship of Yahweh proclaimed in vv. 6–7. But before Israel can fulfill its role of witnessing, it must be forgiven. Second Isaiah always faces squarely the fact that Israel's dormancy is the result of its sin. The sin can be taken away only by Israel's free acceptance of God's forgiveness—hence the imperative to repent in v. 22c.

It is not certain that the invitation to nature to celebrate Yahweh's activity in v. 23 is the beginning of the next passage or the end of the present. Appropriately Yahweh redeems and "has got glory," i.e. found a place on earth where his heavenly glory may be seen—in Israel his witness.

7th Speech

YAHWEH APPOINTS CYRUS KING

[44:24–45:13]

²⁴Thus says Yahweh who redeemed you,
    who fashioned you from the womb.
"It is I, Yahweh, maker of all things,
    who alone stretches out the heavens,
    flattens out the earth—who was with me?
²⁵He nullifies the signs of diviners,
    makes fools of augurs,
thwarts the wise,
    turns their lore into nonsense.
²⁶He establishes the word of his servant,
    fulfills the statement of his messengers.
He says of Jerusalem, 'Be inhabited!'
    of the cities of Judah, 'Be rebuilt!
    I will rebuild your ruins.'
²⁷He says to the Deep, 'Be dry!
    I will dry up your Rivers!'
²⁸He says to Cyrus, 'My shepherd!
    he will do my pleasure,'
will say of Jerusalem, 'Let it be rebuilt;
    let the Temple be refounded.' "[1]

---

1. The syntax of 44:24–28, *'āmar* (finite verb) + participles + *lĕ* + infinitive, occurs also in 49:5. In both cases the syntax makes clear that the action of the human agent expressed by the infinitive, which is dependent on the finite verb of speaking, is done at the behest of Yahweh. Cf. also the similar syntax in 42:6–7 and 49:5, 8.

[45:1]Thus says Yahweh to Cyrus his anointed,
   whose right hand he has grasped,
subduing nations before him,
   ungirding the loins of kings,
opening doors before him;
   no gate will remain shut.
[2]I will march at your head,
   mountains[2] I will level,
doors of bronze I will break down,
   bolts of iron I will slice through.
[3]I will give you treasures lying in darkness,
   hoards in secret places,
so that you may recognize that I am Yahweh,[3]
   the one who calls you by your name,
   the God of Israel.
[4]For the benefit of my servant Jacob,
   Israel my chosen,
I call you by your name;
   I confer your title, though you know me not.
[5]I am Yahweh; there is no other,
   beside me there is no god.
I gird you with authority though you know me not,
[6]that people may recognize from the rising of the sun to its
   setting,
that there is none but me.

---

2. We adopt the reading of the Greek and of the IQIsa[a], *hrrym* for MT *hdrwrym*. The letters *d* and *r* are often confused in the script. For a recent statement and example, see Emanuel Tov, *The Text-Critical Use of the Septuagint in Biblical Research* (Jerusalem Biblical Studies; Jerusalem: Simor, 1981) 289–98.

3. In the section the prophet has a predilection for groups of three: 44:25–26, where the frustrating of the pagan "prophecies" is mentioned in two bicola and the upholding of Israelite prophecy is mentioned in the third; 44:26c–28, where "he says" is repeated three times of divine speech; and 45:1–6, where three times divine action leads to the recognition that Yahweh is God (45:1–3, 4–5b, 5c–6). In the last trio there is a progression; one begins by recognizing that Yahweh is the God behind Cyrus and ends by recognizing that Yahweh is the God who creates all. The last trio prepares the hearer for vv. 9–13 where Israel's unwillingness to acknowledge Cyrus as Yahweh's anointed is reckoned as unwillingness to acknowledge Yahweh as Creator.

I am Yahweh and there is no other,
7   the maker of light and creator of darkness,
   the maker of peace and the creator of evil.
It is I, Yahweh, maker of all things.

8Pour down from above, O heavens,
   let the clouds rain righteousness.
Let the earth open up and bud forth salvation,
   let righteousness blossom forth.
I Yahweh have created it.

9Fool, who fights with the one who made him,
   a pot with the potter.
Does the clay say to the one who shapes it, "What are you
      doing?4
   Your work has no handles"?
10Fool, who says to his father, "What have you begot?"
   to a woman, "What are you bearing?"
11Thus says Yahweh,
   the Holy One of Israel and its maker,
"Will you question me about my children,
   command me about the work of my hands?"
12I made the earth,
   I created man upon it.
I with my hands stretched out the heavens,
   all its host are under my command.5
13I roused him for victory,
   I smooth all his paths.
He will rebuild my city,
   he will lead back my exiled people,
without price and without payment,
   says Yahweh of hosts.

---

4. The question "What are you doing?" is the kind of question that God asks in Gen 4:10, Job 9:12, Dan 4:35, and cf. Qoh 8:4.

5. The totality of creation power is expressed by the familiar merism heaven and earth. Each sphere has a population; people on earth and heavenly beings (or angels) in the heavens.

COMMENTARY

In this speech the word of forgiveness and reconstruction of the opening vision attains a specificity not seen before. The mission of Cyrus is portrayed with a new concreteness, inviting Israel to see the rescuing action of its God in his achievements. Cyrus is to carry out, albeit unwittingly, the will of his patron deity, Yahweh, rebuilding his temple and bringing back his worshipers.

Temple building and festal processions are both acts of ancient Near Eastern kings in response to the god's creation. For Second Isaiah, Cyrus is the typical king; he rebuilds the Temple and brings the people home in procession. The prophet has borrowed from the portrait of the Assyrian king in First Isaiah and of Nebuchadnezzar in Jeremiah.[6] Both prophets portray the typical enemy king, aiming to plunder the temple and exile the people. For First Isaiah and Jeremiah, the king is the unwitting instrument of Yahweh who had decided to punish his people through the empire's depredations. "Ah, Assyria, the rod of my anger, / the staff of my fury. Against an ungodly nation I send him, / against a people of my wrath I command him, / to take spoil and seize plunder, / and to tread them down like mire in the streets. But he does not so intend, / and his mind does not so think /. . . . For he says: "By the strength of my hand I have done it, / and by my wisdom, for I have understanding; / I have erased the boundaries of peoples, / and have plundered their treasuries; / I have exiled their vast populations" (Isa 10:5–7, 13). But now Yahweh is using an empire to restore Israel. Cyrus, unaware like the earlier kings of the ultimate source of his military success, undoes the damage wrought by them. He rebuilds the Temple and causes the people to come home. Israelite refusal to accept Cyrus as Yahweh's-anointed (a term hitherto reserved to Israelite kings and leaders) is reckoned by the prophet as culpable misunderstanding of the nature of Yahweh as the one God who controls all kings and all history.

The unity of the passage is easily demonstrated. There are three

---

6. In First Isaiah the texts are 5:26–30; 7:18–20; 8:5–8; 10:5–19; 10:27d–32; 14:24–27; 30:8–17. In Jeremiah one finds passages in chapters 4–6 on "the enemy from the north" who will be the instrument of divine punishment on Israel. The Babylonian king Nebuchadnezzar is later seen to be the enemy in 21:1–10; 25:8–14; 32:3–5.

stanzas; the first and last of 20 cola each and the middle of 28 cola. V. 8 is probably extra-stanzaic. Each stanza mentions Cyrus, 44:24–28; 45:1–7; vv. 9–13. The ideas and even the outline of the great First Isaian poem on the Assyrian king show their influence on all parts of our poem, some of which have been noted in the above paragraph. The third stanza, 45:9–13, reflects the interjection *hôy,* "Ah," of Isa 10:5 ("Fool" in vv. 9–10). The questions "Does the axe vaunt itself over him who hews with it . . ." etc. of 10:15 are found with slight variation in vv. 9–11. Unfortunately the influence of First Isaiah upon Second Isaiah has been underrated through constant scholarly stress on the separateness of the latter prophet; the correspondence between the Assyrian king and Cyrus has not been sufficiently drawn out.

Fundamental to the first stanza, 44:24–28, is Yahweh's sole divinity which is expressed in the present participles characteristic of hymns. We translate them in accord with English idiom in the third person, e.g., "he says of Jerusalem," but literally the line reads, "who says of Jerusalem . . ." Yahweh speaks in the first person hymnic style after introducing himself as the one who brought Israel into existence "from the womb" (v. 24b). The usual Deutero-Isaian description for the act of creation, "stretching out the heavens" and "flattening out [lit. "hammering flat"] the earth" is elaborated in v. 24de to emphasize that Yahweh is the sole deity: "It is I, Yahweh, maker of all things." Since no other gods were involved in creation, the spokespersons of those deities, diviners, augurs, wise men, have no standing; their statements are empty (v. 25). Yahweh's predictive word uttered by his messengers, on the contrary, powerfully shapes the world.

The specific word in v. 26cde is that Jerusalem and its daughter cities are to be rebuilt and reinhabited. Isa 40:9 had spoken of Jerusalem announcing to the cities of Judah that their God comes; here we see that the coming of the Lord means the rebuilding of the cities. The identical participle, "who says . . ." three times repeated in vv. 26c, 27a and 28a, has the effect of putting all three commands on the same plane. The healing of Jerusalem and nearby cities, the vanquishing of the chaotic waters, and the appointment of Yahweh's king ("my shepherd") are all aspects of the same act. The three linked commands concretize the meaning of the initiating command

"Comfort, comfort my people" of 40:1. Chaotic forces hostile to the existence of the people are to be curbed; the city and the Temple, necessary for peoplehood, are to be rebuilt. Cyrus, successfully destroying the Babylonian Empire, will effect the rebuilding by his own royal decree (v. 28c).

The actual decree of Cyrus to rebuild the Temple is preserved in the Bible. The Hebrew version was apparently posted in the Jewish communities.

> Thus says Cyrus king of Persia: Yahweh the God of heaven has given me all the kingdoms of the earth, and he has charged me to build him a temple at Jerusalem which is in Judah. Whoever is among you of all his people, may his God be with him, and let him go up to Jerusalem which is in Judah and rebuild the temple of Yahweh the God of Israel—he is the God who is in Jerusalem; and let each survivor, in whatever place he sojourns, be assisted by the men of his place with silver and gold, with goods and with beasts, besides freewill offerings for the temple of God which is in Jerusalem.[7]

The decree to rebuild the Temple in Second Isaiah is directly related to the creation victory bringing order from chaos. Ancient Near Eastern creation accounts tell how the god built his temple after conquering chaos and making the world habitable.[8] The temple was the place where the victory was especially manifest, since the god's heavenly glory was visible to people there. By his choosing Cyrus, Yahweh is declaring the Persian to be the instrument of his creation; hence he is the appropriate builder of the Temple. It is significant that the building of the Temple was one of the tasks of the Israelite or any Eastern king. This task is given to Cyrus. Other royal

---

7. Ezra 1:2–4. The authenticity of the decree as a public edict is defended by E. Bickerman, "The Edict of Cyrus in Ezra 1," *JBL* 65 (1956) 246–74. See *ANET,* p. 316 for similar decrees of Cyrus.

8. A temple is built for Marduk after his victory over Tiamat in the Akkadian epic *Enuma elish,* Tablet 7, lines 50–81, English translation in *ANET,* 68–69. In the Ugaritic cycle of Baal, building a temple for Baal is a major concern. The actual temple building is described in *CTA* 4 (*UT* 51), columns 5 and 6, *ANET* 133–34.

functions, particularly that of witness to the nations, are given to the Israelite people.

The next stanza, 45:1–7, underlies the freedom of Yahweh's choice and its result in Cyrus' military success. According to Isaiah 10, Yahweh had sent the Assyrian king to campaign against his own people to take spoil, though "he [the Assyrian king] does not so intend, and his mind does not so think" (10:7). Cyrus too is given booty, "treasures lying in darkness," and is likewise unaware of Yahweh's hand. Cyrus will ultimately recognize Yahweh as the God behind his success (v. 3c), unlike the benighted Assyrian king who thinks to himself, "By the strength of my hand I have done it." Since it is Israel's God who propels Cyrus, the successful campaign has all been for Israel's benefit (v. 4). Recognition of Yahweh as the only deity will not only be by Cyrus and Israel. The whole world is to recognize Yahweh's lordship (vv. 5–6). The stanza ends with a self-proclamation, like that of 44:24–28: Yahweh declares that he controls completely all aspects of creation: light and darkness, order and chaos (the meaning of "evil"). The prophet moves ancient creation thought forward. The usual expression was that God put into their proper sphere chaotic powers such as darkness and formless waters, with no statement as to God's mastery over those forces prior to the creation conflict. Here all is under the one God.

V. 8 is a brief hymn, perhaps to be attached to the third stanza, but more probably not part of the three-stanza structure. It invites the natural world, created in all its parts by the victory of Yahweh, to display that victory. The heavens rain down the waters which, now tamed, give life. The earth, made fertile, now blooms. Both display Yahweh's righteousness, the beautiful order conferred on the world.

Is man able to join with nature in recognizing and applauding the creation victory effected through Cyrus? Israel should be the first to celebrate; after all, its God is the one who conquers. But, as vv. 9–13 imply, it balks. Second Isaiah draws once more on Isaiah 10. First Isaiah had directed his words against the Assyrian king who did not recognize Yahweh's power in his success: "Does the axe [Assyrian king] boast over the one who chops with it [Yahweh]?" (10:15). For Second Isaiah it is the Israelites who fail to recognize Yahweh. The metaphor of the instrument (or the material) question-

ing the actions of the master shows the narrow-minded arrogance of
Israel. It refuses to let Yahweh be the God who does something new.
The cry "alas," which we translate "Fool," in vv. 9a and 10a seems
to be borrowed from Isaiah 10:5. Originally a funerary lament uttered over the corpse—e.g. "Alas, my brother!"—it was borrowed by
the prophets for their preaching. They pronounced it over "death sit-
uations," lamenting in anticipation a situation doomed to fail. People
who no longer believe Yahweh can create are doomed. They are
fools in the biblical sense. Not understanding what it means to have
Yahweh as their God (v. 11ab), they deserve the harsh questions of
v. 11cd.

The discourse ends appropriately with vv. 12–13. Yahweh has
created earth with man, and heaven with heavenly beings (the host).
The dual picture nicely illustrates divine control of the whole world
(v. 12). Mastery over man on earth is shown in the guidance of the
victorious Cyrus (13ab). He will build the Temple for Yahweh and
send the exiles to worship there (v. 13cd). He will not do as a merce-
nary (v. 13c), but because Yahweh controls all the heavenly powers
involved in the clash of empires; that is why his last title is Yahweh
of hosts, i.e. of heavenly beings (cf. v. 12d).

The blueprint for Israel has become three-dimensional. The people is invited to believe in the power of its God, becoming visible in
the person of Cyrus. They are to watch his victory as the victory of
their God, and to allow Cyrus to send them home to celebrate in the
rebuilt Temple.

8th Speech

YAHWEH WILL NOT LEAVE THE HOLY CITY IN RUINS

[45:14–25]

¹⁴Thus says Yahweh,
   "The riches of Egypt, the wealth of Ethiopia,
      Sabeans, men of stature,
   shall cross over to you, shall be yours;
      shall cross, shall follow you in fetters.
   They shall bow down before you,
      reverently address you,
   'Only in *your* midst is God,¹
      there is no other god! '
¹⁵Surely you are a God who conceals yourself,
      God of Israel who brings victory.
¹⁶They are ashamed, they are embarrassed, all of them,
      those who make images walk in shame.
¹⁷Israel has gotten victory through Yahweh,
      victory that is everlasting.
   You shall not be ashamed or embarrassed
      for all ages to come."

¹⁸For thus says Yahweh,
   who creates the heavens—
      he is God!

---

1. The confession that God is in the midst of the city is found also in the Zion songs, Psalms 46, 48 and 76.

Who fashions the earth and makes it,
  he founded it!
Not chaos did he create,
  he fashioned it to be inhabited.
"I am Yahweh; there is no other!
[19]Not in secret did I speak,
  at a site in the land of darkness.
I did not say to the seed of Jacob,
  'In chaos seek me.'[2]
I am Yahweh speaking righteousness,
  pronouncing righteous decrees."

[20]"Come, assemble,
  draw near together, survivors of the nations.
They have no knowledge,
  those who carry their wooden statue,
  who address a god who cannot bring victory.[3]
[21]Come forward and speak,
  prepare your case together.
Who announced this from of old,
  from aforetime declared it?
Was it not I, Yahweh?
  there is no other but me.
A God righteous and saving,
  there is no other but me."

[22]"Turn to me and find salvation,
  all the ends of the earth.
For only I am God; there is no other.
[23]By myself I swear,
  righteousness has gone forth from my lips,
  a word that shall not turn back.
Before me every knee shall bow,
  every tongue shall swear.

---

2. The term is a technical term for seeking the face of Yahweh in a sanctuary, *BDB*, 3b *biqqēš*.
3. The scene is like that of 41:5–7.

²⁴Only in Yahweh, it shall surely[4] be said, are righteousness
    and power.
Unto him shall come and be ashamed,
    all who rage against him.
²⁵In Yahweh shall be vindicated and be glorified,
    the whole seed of Israel."

COMMENTARY

The previous passage designated Cyrus as the divinely commissioned rebuilder of the Temple and the City. This speech of Yahweh
develops the theme of Temple and City; the rebuilt city as the site of
the divine creation will not be left in ruins. It is easy for the English
reader to miss the emphasis given to the holy city in the passage. The
emphatic placement of prepositions with the second singular feminine suffix referring to the city (grammatically feminine) in vv. 14–
17 cannot be reproduced in English. Temples and holy cities had a
significance in connection with creation that no longer generally ob-
tains in Western religious feeling.

That the passage is a unified composition is suggested by several
factors. There are four sections, all of approximately equal length, a
common Hebrew mode of stanza buidling (vv. 14–17, 17 cola; vv.
18–19, 14 cola; vv. 20–21, 15 cola; vv. 22–25, 14 cola). There are a
remarkable number of words or roots of words repeated throughout:
hitpallēl, "pray, address fervently," in vv. 14g and 20e; *str,* "be hidden, secret," in vv. 15a, 19a; *yšᶜ,* "to save, be victorious," in vv. 15b,
17ab, 20e, 21g, 22a; *ṣdq,* "be righteous, reliable," in vv. 19e, 21g, 23b,
24a, 25a; *bwš,* "be ashamed," in vv. 16a, 17c, 24c. A single theme is
developed: the holy residence of Yahweh renders his glory visible to
the nations. There is a single scene, sketched with a glance at models
like Isa 2:1–4 on the one hand and Psalms 72 and 149 on the other.
The Isaian text foresees the day when the nations of the world will
hear the authoritative voice of the true God on Mount Zion and
stream toward it. From the Psalms is derived the tradition of the defeated enemy kings forced to bring tribute. There is a consistent emphasis on Zion as the holy place because it is the site of the creation

---

4. We read *lū yē'āmēr* for MT *lî 'āmar.*

victory. Hence, by structure, recurring vocabulary, theme and tradition, Isa 44:14-25 is a single speech.

The first stanza, vv. 14-17, a divine speech like the rest of the poem, describes the tribute brought from exotic lands. The speech of the peoples, vv. 14h-17, a single speech despite the shifting of grammatical person, reveals why they have become vassals. The people have left their own lands and cities to come here (the nuance of "cross over"), for they have concluded that the God of the city and land provides victory for his worshipers. They see that Israel's eclipse was not due to the weakness of its God but to his deliberately hiding himself. But now the city and temple, rebuilt by his king Cyrus, display that long hidden power. The people experience salvation in this holy sphere. The nations admit that they are ashamed and confused; they have seen the things they counted on publicly exposed as empty. To experience the importance of their own gods, and the victory of the god of another people, shocks the visitors into confessing that Israel's God has indeed saved his people. Unlike themselves, the people of Yahweh will never know the embarrassment of its God's impotence to rescue them in crisis.

The Gentile confession should not be exaggerated. They are not incorporated into the tribes of Judah. They rather bring the gifts appropriate to a deity who has shown himself triumphant. The proof of God's triumph is the holy city populated with his worshipers. The nations have been defeated; they come in chains and bear tribute. In v. 20 they are called "survivors," a word always used of those who have survived a military defeat. Either Psalm 72, or a song like it, has influenced the picture. Israel's victory has dethroned its enemies.

In the next stanza, vv. 18-19, Yahweh vigorously restates the nations' confession. He proclaims himself Creator by the customary merism, "creating the heavens" and "fashioning the earth." Expansion of the formula fits it to this context. The phrase "he founded it" describes both the founding of the earth and the founding of Jerusalem (Pss 48:8 and 87:5) and of his sanctuary (Exod 15:17). After his act the world is no longer chaos, i.e. uninhabitable land. "He fashioned it to be inhabited" (v. 18g). He did not speak, i.e. present himself to the people whom he created "in secret," at a site in the "land of darkness" (v. 19ab). The parallel phrases qualify one another. "In secret" means what is not public and open. The word for "site" (mā-

qôm) can mean "shrine," hence the opposite of "land of darkness." Chaos and darkness characterize the world in which Yahweh has not yet triumphed by his creation. To paraphrase v. 19ab positively: I revealed myself to my people openly as befits one who has triumphed, in the shrine which has been established as the opposite of chaotic darkness.

The rest of v. 19 continues the same thought. Yahweh's dwelling reflects his victory over chaos. His command to his people, "Seek me!" means "Come and worship at my Temple!" One is invited to enter the very opposite of chaos. The Temple is the place where God utters his words which insure that the created order will work according to divine intent. The divine intention establishing the world is called righteousness and justice. Kings, legates of the divine will in the establishment of cosmos, customarily published law codes upon their accession to the throne, implementing the same divine justice. The words of justice are spoken appropriately from his house which he builds after his victory.

From the secure site of cosmic victory, and of just governance of the universe, Yahweh can summon the nations of the world. They come, carrying the symbols of their gods, the wooden statues. Like previous scenes of divine questioning (41:1–4, 21–28; 43:9–13; 44:7–8), the scene begins with the question: "Who spoke and then acted according to those words?" The answer is "Yahweh alone!" The words are the old promises which predicted that Yahweh would triumph over his enemies, would be a saving God. The pathetic "survivors of the nations" with their wooden statues are like children with dolls—a dramatic contrast to Yahweh's fidelity to his people.

In the fourth stanza, vv. 22–25, Yahweh calls on people all over the world to turn to him in his holy dwelling where his victory can be experienced. Since he alone made the earth and all its people, the just order of creation demands that all worship him alone, bow down before him and use his name in oaths. Their confession is like the confession of the first stanza, except that the nations use the name Yahweh explicitly. The stock of Israel (v. 25b) will be justified, i.e. will share in the original justice found in Jerusalem. It will be glorified (the opposite of feeling ashamed) in the glory of its God.

In this passage Second Isaiah develops his conception of Zion. As the site of the Temple, it is the place where cosmic victory took place, where Yahweh's power is displayed, and where the same power protects his people. It is inconceivable therefore that it remain in ruins, and its inhabitants scattered. As Gerhard von Rad has said of 44:24–28: "Yahweh the creator, who raised the world up out of chaos, does not leave Jerusalem in chaos; he who dried up the elemental waters will also raise up Jerusalem anew."[5] The divine justice uttered over the created world will be restored and become visible to all.

The prophet here for the first time speaks at length of Zion, the goal of Israel's journey. In the opening vision, we heard that Jerusalem will be the goal of pilgrimage and will in fact announce the coming of Yahweh to surrounding towns. During the course of the prophecy we have come to learn how Jerusalem will be rebuilt, and now we hear why it will be rebuilt. Gradually the message "comfort my people" is becoming more explicit. Yahweh will never leave his holy city, his dwelling in ruins. It has to become the site of the power that conquers darkness and the folly of other gods. It is the milieu in which Israel is to live.

5. "The Theological Problem of the Old Testament Doctrine of Creation," in *The Problem of the Hexateuch and Other Essays* (New York: McGraw-Hill, 1966; German original 1936), 136.

9th Speech

YAHWEH CARRIES HIS PEOPLE TO HIS CITY

[46]

¹Bel bows down, Nebo dips low,
on beasts and cattle are they borne,
carried, a burden on exhausted animals.¹
²They dip low, they bow down.
They are not able to bring their burden to safety,
they themselves march into captivity.
³Listen to me, O house of Jacob,
all the remnant of the house of Israel,
you who have been carried since birth,
borne since leaving the womb.
⁴Unto old age I am he,
when you turn gray, I will still carry.
I have acted and I will bear,
I will carry and I will bring to safety.

⁵To whom will you liken me, make me equal,
to whom will you compare me that we may be like?²

---

1. We read *kr ᶜbl qrs nbw / lhyh wlbhmh nś't / mwswt mś' l'yph / qrsw kr'w yhdw*.
I suggest that a gloss, *hāyû 'ăsabbêhem*, "They were their idols," was taken into the
body of the text at an early stage and seemed to early interpreters (LXX and Targum)
to be the prose idiom, "to become." For further details, see my "The Function of Idol
Passages in Second Isaiah," *CBQ* 42 (1980) 455, fn. 19.

2. As in similar questions in Second Isaiah, the answer is a specific portrait of the
makers of images, 41:5–7, 40:18–20 and 44:12–17.

⁶Those who lavish gold from their purse,
    who weigh out silver on the scales,
  hire a smith to make a god
    for people to adore and worship.³
⁷They bear it on their shoulders and carry it,
    they set it on its base, it stands upright;
  from its base it cannot be moved.
  ['ap]⁴ One cries out to it but it does not respond;
    from his troubles it does not save him.

⁸Remember this and consider [?],
    take this to heart, you rebels.
⁹Remember the first events, from olden days,
  I am God, there is no other,
    there is none like me, God.
¹⁰I am he who tells from the first events yet to come,
    from of old what has not yet taken place;
  who states my plan that will take effect,
    my good pleasure that will be done;⁵
¹¹who calls from the east a bird of prey,
    from a far off land a man to do my will.
  ['ap] I have spoken: I will bring it to pass.
  I have purposed; I will do it.
¹²Listen to me, you stubborn of heart,
    you who are far from justice.
¹³I have made my justice present; it is not far off;
    my victory does not delay.
  I have put victory in Zion,
    to Israel I have given my glory.

---

3. Not "then they fall down and worship," since this translation would interrupt the unified action of a single person hiring a smith at great cost and carrying the statue home. Like the similar usage in 44:15, 17, 19, the third personal plural masculine verb is used for the passive (*GKC* §144f).

4. The Hebrew word *'ap* repeated in v. 11 underlines the contrast between the static statue made by man and the dynamic man.

5. Reading with IQIsaᵃ *yᶜšh*.

COMMENTARY

Though it may not immediately appear to do so, chapter 46 continues the theme of Zion, or, more accurately, the relation of Babylon and Zion to their respective divine patrons. It is entirely an address of Yahweh to his people, combining two dramatic cameos, vv. 1–2 and vv. 4–7, and self-proclamation, vv. 3–4 and 8–11. That it is a single composition is demonstrated by the clear pairing of favorite Deutero-Isaian polarities: Zion and Babylon (in the person of Bel and Nebo), Yahweh and Bel and Nebo, the exiled Israelites and the exiled Babylonians. The polarities are partly expressed by key words: "carry" and "bear" used of pack animals carrying images of gods and Yahweh carrying Israel; "to bring to safety, escape (most often from a destroyed city)" used to describe the activity of Bel and Nebo as well as of Yahweh.

It is not easy to point to a clear outline. One must rely on the sense, conveyed by the polarities and the repetition of the plural imperatives "hear" and "remember."

1. vv. 1–4, 15 cola.   Babylon's gods cannot rescue their people from destruction. Yahweh ever rescues and carries his people to safety.

2. vv. 5–7, 11 cola.   Yahweh's lordship is like that of no other gods, which are made by human beings and, being static, cannot save.

vv. 8–13, 21 cola.   Yahweh places his saving power in his city.

The logic of the discourse is not difficult. Vv. 1–2 are a dramatization: pack animals carry statues of the Babylonian gods, Bel and Nebo. They are part of the general flight from the destroyed city, as is implied in v. 2bc. They are unable to save their worshipers. The Babylonians' going into exile carrying their gods (vv. 1–2) is the background against which the Israelites are addressed by their God in vv. 3–4. They are called the "remnant" of the house of Israel suggesting that Israel as exiled is contrasted with Babylon as exiled.

Two tableaux are compared: refugees from Babylon and refugees from Zion. What is each group's relation to its patron god(s)?

Second Isaiah has summoned up two pictures of people with their gods which provide him with rich contrasts for his preaching. The technique of parallel scenes is well known in Hebrew rhetoric and has been discussed in chapter 2.

Israel is addressed in vv. 3–4. Yahweh has carried them from birth, and will continue carrying them till old age. The verb "to bear" *(nāśā')* has been used for the tender care of the divine shepherd in 40:11, and the famous passage of Yahweh protecting his own in Exod 19:4; Deut 32:11 and Ps 91:2. Here the verb not only evokes the traditional use but also alludes ironically to the Babylonian pack animals. Even more important, the verbs of carrying suggest that Yahweh will carry his people to a restored city, Zion. The importance of the city will be made explicit in vv. 12–13.

Yahweh's kingship in the heavens is elsewhere expressed by the rhetorical question, "Who is like Yahweh among the gods?"[6] The answer to the question is of course "no one." To demonstrate that conclusion one must eliminate in argument rival claimants—the other gods represented by their statues. So in 40:18–19, "To whom will you compare God . . .? A statue! A craftsman casts it . . ."; and later in the same passage, "To whom will you compare . . .? Raise your eyes to heaven. See who created them [members of the heavenly army]." In our passage the rhetorical questions are aimed at eliminating rival claimants to Israel's allegiance by ridiculing their images. As in 44:12–17, the speech simply describes the actions of the votaries of the gods, allowing the reader to see for himself the irony. The worshipers themselves have a statue made at great expense which then has to be carried and secured to a base. It cannot speak or act to benefit its makers. Yahweh on the contrary acts, carrying his people from birth.

The next stanza, vv. 8–11, begins with a harsh summons to the rebels to remember the mighty acts of old. The rebels are those exiled Israelites who have refused to acknowledge that their God has carried them in the past and is about to carry them in the future. By

---

6. E.g. Exod 15:11 and Ps 89:6.

refusing to let themselves be carried by him, they put him in the same category as the static gods who cannot carry their people.

To remember the first events (v. 8c, essentially the Creation/Exodus-Conquest) means to encounter Yahweh's very self, the divine "I" which is the subject of vv. 9–11. These ancient deeds show that Yahweh alone is God. His sole divinity is expressed in present participles of speaking and acting in accord with his divine nature. Like the sequence of participles in 44:24–28, the series in vv. 9–11 moves from the statement of sole divinity ("I am God") to participles expressing divine speaking and acting, climaxing in the call of Cyrus, the "bird of prey." "Bird of prey" apparently alludes to passages such as Isa 18:6, Jer 12:9 and Ezek 39:4, where carrion birds and wild animals are called to feast on Yahweh's enemies. Cyrus is not only the builder of Jerusalem; he is also the destroyer of Babylon, as the first verses of this chapter and the entire next chapter remind us.

The last address to Israel is harsh, branding them as stubborn and "far from my justice." "Far from my justice" is not mere metaphor; it describes the actual physical state of "the remnant of the house of Israel" (v. 3b). They are in Babylon, far from Zion where Yahweh has chosen to dwell and to speak his words that give order to the world, i.e. his "justice" and his "salvation." "I have made my justice present" in v. 13a is a Hebrew idiom meaning "I have brought it in the sanctuary." As 45:18–25 stated so eloquently, Yahweh does not permit his dwelling to be without the justice and salvation proper to it as a place of creation. The destruction of Babylon and the flight of its helpless gods send a clear message to Israel: do not keep yourselves distant from the shrine of God, Zion.

10th Speech

THE DESTRUCTION OF DAME BABYLON

[47]

¹Get down, sit in the dust,
  Fair Maiden Babylon.
Sit upon the ground—there is no throne—
  Fair Chaldea.
For no longer will they call you
  delicate and refined.
²Take up the millstone, grind meal,
  remove your veil.
Strip off your train,
  bare your leg,
  cross the rivers.
³Your nakedness will be uncovered,
  your shame will be exposed.
I will take vengeance,
  let no one dissuade me.
⁴The one who redeems us—Yahweh of hosts is his name,
  the Holy One of Israel.
⁵Sit in silence, go into the darkness,
  Fair Chaldea.
For no longer will they call you
  mistress of kingdoms.

⁶I was angry at my people,
  I cast out my possession as profane.

I gave them into your hands,
    you showed them no pity,
upon the old you made your yoke exceedingly heavy.
[7]You said, "I will exist forever,
    mistress always."
You did not keep this in mind,
    you gave no thought to its final end.

[8]And now hear this, indulgent one
    who lived without a care;
who thought to yourself,
    "I am, there is no other.
I will never be a widow,
    never know bereavement of children."
[9]Both shall come upon you,
    in a flash, in a single day.
Loss of children and widowhood with full force
    shall come upon you
despite your many sorceries,
    despite the great power of your enchantments.

[10]You felt secure in your wickedness,
    you said, "No one has power over me."[1]
Your wisdom and your lore,
    these provided sufficient guidance.[2]
You thought to yourself,
    "I am, there is no other."
[11]Upon you will come evil,
    you will not know how to avert it by a bribe.
Upon you will fall disaster,
    you will not be able to buy it off.

---

1. The context suggests that the Hebrew idiom *rā'â bĕ,* "to gloat over (fallen enemies)," should be read into MT *rō'ānî.*

2. Context suggests that *šôbĕbātēk,* which most translations take as "led you astray" or the like, should be taken in its meaning of "refresh, restore." The whole of v. 10 quotes the arrogant boasting of the queen who would scarcely admit to having been led astray.

Upon you there will come, suddenly,
    destruction you never suspected.

¹²Stand up then with your enchantments,
    with your many sorceries
on which you have spent yourself since youth.
Perhaps you will derive benefit,
    perhaps you will be able to inspire respect,
¹³   by your many strategies which have drained your energy.

Let them stand forth and give you victory,
    the scanners of the heavens,
    the gazers at the stars,
those who announce month by month
    what shall come upon you.³
¹⁴They are so much chaff,
    the flame burns them.
They are not able to save themselves
    from the power of the hearth.
This is no fire to warm oneself by,
    a flame to sit before.
¹⁵So they have ended up—those with whom you have toiled,
    your trading partners from your youth.
Each moves aimlessly on his own path,
    none of them can give victory.

COMMENTARY

This taunt song over ruined Babylon continues in an indirect way the theme of Zion that began to be developed in detail in Cyrus' commission to rebuild the city in 44:24–45:13. For Babylon is the counter-image of Zion the holy city. Babylon's brief ascendancy, willed by Yahweh for the sake of Israel (v. 6), is now definitively ended, again for Israel's benefit. Babylon is told to descend to the

---

3. V. 11 had predicted disaster would come upon Babylon, twice using the Hebrew phrase *bô' 'al* "come upon." The useless diviners "come upon" Babylon. They are the partial cause of her downfall.

ground in v. 1 whereas Jerusalem was told to ascend a mountain in 40:9. Babylon's silence contrasts with Jerusalem's proclamation that her Lord is coming. Babylon's "lords" have already departed in the person of Bel and Nebo (chapter 46). A city is holy because of the presence of her god (sometimes conceived of as her husband), and because she is the site of encounter between her god and his worshipers. The worshipers are often conceived of as her children.[4] Zion's "divorce" from her husband is about to be reversed (50:1), and her children are about to stream back.[5] Before Zion's restoration, Babylon's double deprivation, widowhood and loss of children (vv. 8–9), must first take place. Babylon is dethroned. Israel no longer has any excuse for remaining in the doomed city. The way is prepared for the urgent call to return to Zion in 48:20–22, repeated many times thereafter. The themes of the chapter are thus integral to the book.

Much of the material of the chapter is traditional. Ezek 27:1–36 is a similar taunt against the maritime power, Tyre. Personified as a ship laden with wares, Tyre is sunk by the very sea which once brought it wealth. Other taunt songs are directed against the rulers who personify the self-sufficiency and arrogance of the city-state: the prince of Tyre in Ezek 28:1–10 and vv. 11–19, and the king of Babylon in Isa 14:3–21. A taunt is meant to be sung by the enemy when the city is destroyed: where now all the vaunted resources used to dominate others? Modern Westerners generally do not regard public ridicule of defeated enemies as admirable but it was part of the conventions of the ancient taunt genre. One need only recall the scorn eloquently uttered by the Homeric hero over his fallen enemy. Moreover there was question of reaffirming divine justice. Babylon was guilty of *public* injustice; there had to be public divestment of all insignia of sinful power. Because it is Yahweh who taunts, the song becomes by that fact a judgment scene in which Babylon is found guilty of transgressing the divine plan which had made it Yahweh's instrument (vv. 6–7). Despite the knowledge it boasted of, it had not recognized Yahweh as the only God. It rather claimed that title for

4. For materials and bibliography on the personification of cities in the ancient East, see Aloysius Fitzgerald, "The Mythological Background for the Presentation of Jerusalem as Queen and False Worship in the OT," *CBQ* 34 (1972) 403–16 and "*Btwlt* and *Bt* as Titles for Capital Cities," *CBQ* 37 (1975) 167–83.

5. Chapter 49, especially vv. 12, 18, 20, 21–22.

itself (vv. 8d and 10f). As it had earlier against the nations whose gods made such claims for themselves (41:1–42:9), a divine word reveals the emptiness of the Babylonian claim. Once again, the prophet has recast freely an old genre.

The chapter itself can be divided into the following stanzas, admittedly more on the basis of sense than on formal considerations: vv. 1–5, 6–7, 8–9, 10–11, 12–13a, 13b–15.

The voice of Yahweh dominates vv. 1–5, demanding that the great queen divest herself of her royal privileges and become a grinding slave, deprived of voice, her person demeaned. Jerusalem had been told in 40:9–11 to ascend to a mountain and proclaim with royal freedom the good news of victory. Yahweh is "our Redeemer," i.e., the one whose love and sense of honor lead him to rescue his family and punish his enemies.

Vv. 6–7 elaborate with regard to Babylon the First Isaian interpretation of Assyria in 10:5–9: the empire is the instrument of Yahweh's anger against his people but soon exceeds the mandate. The tyrant interprets his success as due to his own strength. Cruelty toward the defenseless, especially toward the elderly in v. 6, characterizes the tyrant. The "final end," v. 7d, which Babylon did not attend to, is a biblical idiom meaning the final term in a series of actions which provides a perspective for right judgment of those actions. Psalm 73 illustrates the general perspective provided by "the end." "But as for me, my feet had almost stumbled . . . when I saw the prosperity of the wicked . . . then I perceived their end . . . How they are destroyed in a moment, swept away utterly by terrors" (vv. 2, 3, 17, 19 RSV). Babylon in v. 7ab had just claimed deity, "I will exist forever, mistress for always," but it does not know, "the end," the true perspective. Its claim therefore is fraudulent.

Sentence is pronounced against the queen in vv. 8–9. The loss of her claims to glory—her marriage to her gods and her throng of citizen-worshipers—will be destroyed in a single moment. Her claims of being forever powerful (vv. 8def) and hence divine (only gods were eternal) turn out to be empty. Her knowledge, gained from divination, is proven entirely inadequate. She "thought," (v. 8c) "I will never *know* bereavement" (v. 8f). It is shown to be useless in the day of disaster.

Vv. 10–11 repeat vv. 8–9 but underline the inadequacy of the foreknowledge of Babylon. In the first three bicola of v. 10, the speaker describes Babylon boasting of her knowledge. In the three bicola of the next verse, v. 11, marked by three prepositions with second singular feminine suffix,[6] disaster overtakes the city. Three times it is stated that Babylon the wealthy merchant city does not *know how* to buy off disaster, is not able to fend it off by bribes, has no idea of it.

The destruction that comes upon the city is at the same time divine judgment. Hence in vv. 12–13a the queen must stand in the docket before her judge. She is allowed "benefit of counsel," the vaunted sources of knowledge, the diviners, which, it turns out, have drained away her strength.

The last stanza, vv. 13b–15, is a final summons for Babylon and those upon whom she relied to come forward. Her helpers have proven to be useless chaff, helpless before the flame that consumes them. Babylon's props—her trading partners and her wise men—are unable to help her as she descends from her throne and crosses rivers on her way to the lands of her exile (v. 1). They too leave the city for a variety of destinations. They cannot bring victory in the crisis brought by Yahweh's judgment.

The prophet has already announced Yahweh as the builder of Jerusalem (44:24–45:13), has declared that his divine justice will not allow the city to remain in ruins and chaos (45:14–25), has shown Yahweh to be the ever-reliable carrier of his people (chapter 46). He now declares the destruction of "counter-Zion." Those upon whom she relied cannot sustain her. She is bereft of husband and children at a single stroke. The way is prepared for "counter-Babylon" Zion to be sustained with Yahweh's presence once again and to be filled with her worshiping children.

---

6. The threefold repetition is reminiscent of 45:14.

11th Speech

OPENNESS TO THE INTERPRETING WORD

[48]

[1]Hear this, O house of Jacob,
who call yourselves Israel,
who have come forth from Judah's loins;[1]
You who take oaths by Yahweh's name,
who invoke the God of Israel—
neither validly nor fittingly!
[2]For you call yourselves after the holy city.
On the God of Israel do you lean,
Yahweh of hosts is his name.

[3]The first events, in time of old, I announced,
from my mouth they issued, I declared them,
suddenly I acted, they came to pass.
[4]Because I know how stubborn you are—
your neck is an iron sinew,
your forehead, brass—
[5]I announced to you long beforehand,
before it took place, I declared it to you,
so you could not say, "My idol did it,
my statue directed it."
[6]You heard, saw everything,
do you not admit this?

---

1. We read *mm'y* for MT *mmy*.

I declare new things at the present time,
 well-guarded secrets you did not know.
[7]Now they are created, not in the time of old,
 before today,[2] you have not heard them,
  so you could say, "I already knew it."
[8]You have not heard, you have not known,
 your ears were not opened hitherto.
For I know how traitorous you are,
 that you are called a rebel from the womb.

[9]For the sake of my name I restrain my anger,
 for my renown I rein it in,
  so as not to exterminate you.
[10]I have refined you, not like silver,
 I tested you in the furnace of affliction.
[11]For my sake, for my sake, I act.
 For how can I profane my name?[3]
My glory I will not give to another.

[12]Hear me, O Jacob,
 Israel whom I call.
I am the One, am the first,
 Yes, I am the last.
[13]Yes, my hand founded the earth,
 my right hand spread out the heavens.
I call to them,
 let them stand forth all together.
[14]Let them all assemble and hear.
 Who among you announced these things?
Yahweh loves him,
 he will carry out his will against Babylon,
  his might against Chaldea.
[15]It is I, I am the one who has spoken, have called him,
 I have brought him, and made his way prosper.

---

2. Literally "before day." Obscure. We take it as parallel to "well guarded secrets" in v. 6d. The full parallel is 6cd/7ab.
3. We add "my name" from Greek.

[16]Draw near to me, hear this.
In time of old I did not speak in secret,
in the very time when it happened, I was there.[4]
Now the Lord Yahweh has sent me, endowed with his spirit.
[17]Thus says Yahweh your Redeemer,
the Holy One of Israel.
I am Yahweh your God,
who teaches you what profits,
who causes you to walk on the way you should go.
[18]If only you would heed my authoritative words,
your prosperity would be like a river,
your triumph like the waves of the sea.
[19]Your progeny would be as many as the sand,
the issue of your loins as many as its grains.
Their names would not be obliterated,
not cut off from my presence.

[20]Go forth from Babylon,
flee from Chaldea.
Announce with jubilant voice,
declare it.
Publish the word
to the ends of the earth.
Say, "Yahweh has redeemed
his servant Jacob!"
[21]They thirsted not
when he led them through parched places.
Water from the rock
he made flow for them.
He split the rock,
there flowed out water.
[22][Prosperity is not for the wicked, says Yahweh.][5]

---

4. I.e. with my word, as can be inferred from the parallel. Also see the case made for the association of word and deed in vv. 3–6. So also *NJV* note, "i.e. I sent prophets; cf. 45:19."

5. V. 21 seems to be a gloss that denies to the wicked a share in the prosperity (*šālōm*) of v. 18.

COMMENTARY

The speech is concerned with the holy cities of Babylon and Zion less directly than the preceding material. The emphasis falls rather on the "precondition for knowing," as a modern philosopher might put it: what Israel must do to recognize the authentic power of God.

What Israel must do is wait for the interpretive word which accompanies any divine act. And that word, delivered by the mysterious messenger of v. 16d, declares that the "new event" begins with Cyrus' attack on the Babylonian Empire. Israel's future prosperity, vv. 17–19, depends on its obedience now to the command to flee Babylon, vv. 22–24.

The argument for unity of composition rests on more than the logic of the précis just given; there are also formal indicators. The same word, "to call," "to call oneself, to be known as," with a human as subject, occurs in vv. 1b, 2a, 8d, in clear and deliberate contrast to its use later in the poem, "to call, summon," with Yahweh as subject in vv. 12b, 13c, and 15a. The root $\check{s}m^c$ occurs frequently, with the meaning "to hear" in vv. 1a, 6a, 12a, 16a, and in the causative conjugation meaning "to announce" in vv. 3b, 5b, 6c, illustrating, it seems, concern for obedience to the word proclaimed. Beyond word distribution, vv. 1–11 (38 cola) seem to be parallel to vv. 12–21 (37 cola). The first half of the speech bids Jacob to hear (vv. 1–2) because, in view of Israel's stubbornness, a divine word always accompanies the divine deed, whether of the past or of now (vv. 3–8). Yahweh's zeal for his own name lies behind all activity (vv. 9–11). The second half of the speech, vv. 12–21, bids Jacob to hear (v. 12ab), reiterates the link between divine word and deed (vv. 12c–13), and declares that the new deed is Cyrus' mission to Babylon accompanied by the word given through "me, endowed with his spirit" (vv. 14–16). Vv. 17–19, like vv. 9–11, restate the persistent divine purpose which is always intent on good even in the face of Israelite obstinacy.

Analysis of the two main sections will further support the claim that there is a coherent message in chapter 48. The customarily brief designation of the addressees, Jacob and Israel, has been expanded several-fold in vv. 1–2. Israel is addressed precisely as the people whose worship of Yahweh (instanced by their swearing by the name and their invocation of God, v. 1de) is seriously flawed. Why it is flawed is revealed explicitly in vv. 1f-2a which stand in clear opposition to v. 1. The phrase in v. 21, literally, "but from the holy city are they called," seems to be a condensed way of saying that the people are to be known by the city of their origin, the city of God, just as any person is known by the city from which he hails. The related phrase "the God of Israel" in the very next colon, v. 2b, suggests that Israel's God is so intimately bound to his city that he is not "validly or fittingly" worshiped outside of it. Second Isaiah is not denying here that Israel's worship during their exile in Babylon was valid. Ezekiel had said that Yahweh himself had become a "mini-sanctuary" in the land of exile, and Jeremiah had told the people to settle down peacefully in Babylon and wait seventy years till their return.[6] But both prophets meant temporary measures in view of eventual return to the land. For Second Isaiah the time of return is now, under the patronage of Cyrus. Hence the people's place of origin, the city of God, has begun to exercise such a powerful claim upon them that worship now in any other place is invalid and unfitting.

The argument of the next section (vv. 3–5), that Yahweh speaks a word authenticating his action that will follow, is familiar enough, but the nuance that *word* precedes *deed* because of Israel's stubbornness is new. Unless a divine prediction verified the deed as Yahweh's, so the prophet says, Israel would credit their idols with the deed, vv. 3–6a. Some scholars deny these and other rebuking passages to Second Isaiah on the grounds he was a prophet of weal not of woe. This judgment is based upon an impossibly rigid preconception that prophets are classed as weal or woe prophets. The rebuke here is entirely appropriate to the passage, giving point to the challenge of vv. 12–19. The "first events" of v. 3 are chiefly the old saving deeds, Creation/Exodus-Conquest. The "announcements" are the words that accompany them, e.g. the promise of progeny and land to the patriarchs that materialize fully only with the conquest, or the plagues against Egypt that take place only after Moses' word.

Having stated in vv. 5–6b the link between ancient deeds and words and its necessity because of the people's stubbornness, the prophet in vv. 6c–8 speaks about contemporary deeds and words.

---

6. Ezek 11:6 and Jer 25:11; 27:7 and chapter 29.

There is no great act of God without a predictive word to clarify its nature. Without the prophetic word Israel has no means of recognizing a divine act or of knowing its nature. Israel cannot know it *a priori;* it must wait for the word and be ready for whatever that word declares. The prophet insists because of Israel's inclination to say "I know it already," and hence deny as divine all acts contrary to its own expectations and biases. Second Isaiah insists that the new action of God, "well guarded secrets you did not know," is only now revealed. The prophet is preparing the people to accept Cyrus' work as the new event, announced by the prophet (vv. 14–16).

Vv. 9–11, though negative upon first reading, are actually a guarantee that Yahweh's work will proceed irrespective of the popular response. That work is founded on Yahweh's zeal for his own name, i.e. that his earthly representative adequately reflect the true grandeur that he has in heaven. V. 10 states that Israel's present distress is not an argument against Yahweh's sovereignty; its distress is due to his deliberate testing of them, as in Egypt.

In the second parallel section, vv. 12–19, the prophet exploits the general reasoning of the first section to make clear that Cyrus is doing the new deed and that he, the prophet, is providing the word. In vv. 12–13 Israel hears again the familiar summary of the first events, the creating of heaven and earth, told with an emphasis on the total subordination of the elements to the word of God. Earth includes, of course, its human inhabitants who, in vv. 13c–14b, are summoned to assembly. Such assemblies have been seen before,[7] so the prophet can reduce this one to its bare essentials, questions about divine control of history. Who on earth, owing his entire existence to Yahweh, would dare on his own to predict and interpret what deed Yahweh now intends to do? Yahweh has chosen[8] Cyrus to act against Babylon and guarantees his success (vv. 14c–15). Regarding the first saving events, those of old, Yahweh spoke publicly and audibly (not . . . in secret," v. 16b). Now, v. 16d, a word will likewise be spoken by a spirit-endowed individual. Here the prophet modestly mentions himself as an individual for the second time, the first men-

7. Isa 43:9–12 and 44:6–9.
8. In the biblical idiom "to love" implies choice, e.g. Ps 78:68: "but he chose the tribe of Judah,/Mount Zion, which he loves."

tion being in 40:6. In other references to himself, he is allied with a group who are intent upon carrying out the will of God.

To an Israel now aware that Cyrus is initiating the new deed Yahweh introduces himself under the familiar title of Redeemer and Holy One, and further the one who shows them the way to prosperity ("what profits," "the right path," v. 17de). Oh that Israel would attend to "my authoritative words" that lead to its prosperity! The word "my authoritative words" has a Deutero-Isaian nuance. In 45:12d and 48:5d the verb of the same root means to give authoritative direction. It is reasonable to conclude that the prophet who otherwise avoids references to the Mosaic covenant[9] uses the word for "commandment" in a special sense. Openness to the divine directive brings prosperity and progeny, i.e. "not being cut off," in the biblical idiom. Prosperity and progeny were promised to the landless and childless patriarchs in Gen 22:17 and 32:12. Their progeny too were to be like the sands of the sea.

The way has been prepared for the direct commands of vv. 20–21. Israel has heard that a new event is interpreted by a new word to which they must be open. The new event is initiated by Cyrus' action against Babylon and announced by the prophet. But the people are called not only to believe but to act. The imperatives of vv. 20–21 summon them to action. Leave the city of the no-gods with exultation appropriate to a victory by Yahweh! Their talk to each on the way is to be of their redemption. The prosperity and righteousness promised in v. 18bc will be felt even in the infertile desert as they journey to the land of promise, v. 21.

---

9. For discussion of the prophet's use of the Mosaic covenant, see B. W. Anderson, "Exodus and Covenant in Second Isaiah and Prophetic Tradition," in *Magnalia Dei: The Mighty Acts of God* (G. E. Wright Volume; ed. F. M. Cross *et al.*; Garden City: Doubleday, 1976) 339–60.

12th Speech

THE SERVANT PERFORMS HIS TASK IN THE SIGHT OF THE NATIONS

[49]

¹Hear me, coastlands,
    attend, O far off nations!
Yahweh called me from the womb,
    from the body of my mother he pronounced my name.
²He made my mouth like a sharp sword,
    in the shadow of his hand he concealed me.
He made me a sharpened arrow,
    in his quiver he hid me.
³He said to me, "You are my servant,
    Israel—in whom I will be glorified."
⁴But I said, "I have labored in vain,
    for nothing and for naught I have spent my strength.¹
But my case is with Yahweh,
    my recompense is with my God."
⁵And now Yahweh has said,
    the one who fashioned me from the womb to be his
        servant,

---

1. "I have labored," "I have spent my strength," *yāga'tî.* The root, along with similar words expressing exhaustion, occurs in 40:28–31, a passage in which Yahweh promises to impart his strength to exhausted Israel.

to restore Jacob to him,[2]
    that Israel might assemble around him.
Hence I have found honor in the eyes of Yahweh,
    my God has become my strength.
[6]He said to me, "It is too slight for you to be my servant
    who is to establish the tribes of Jacob,
    restore the survivors of Israel.
I have made you a light to the nations,
    that my salvation may reach to the ends of the earth."
[7]Thus says Yahweh,
    the Redeemer of Israel, its Holy One,
to one whose being is despised,
    whose body is detested,[3]
    to a servant of rulers.
Kings shall see and stand up,
    princes, and they shall bow down,
because of Yahweh who is faithful,
    the Holy One of Israel who has chosen you.
[8]Thus says Yahweh,
In a time of favor I have responded to you,
    in a day of victory I have come to your aid.
I fashioned you and made you a covenant to the peoples,
    to settle the land,
    to distribute the destroyed land allotments;
[9]to say to the prisoners, "Go free!"
    to those who are in darkness, "Show yourselves!"
Along the road they shall feed,
    on the bare heights will be their pasture.
[10]They will neither hunger nor thirst,
    hot wind and sun will not strike them.

---

2. The syntax is important for showing that a subordinate figure is commissioned to do Yahweh's work, *ʾāmar . . . lĕ ʿebed lô lĕšôbēb*. It is identical to v. 8def, *wĕʾ ettenkā librît ʿām lĕhāqîm ʾeres* (and v. 9ab), and to 42:6–7 and to 44:24–28. Yahweh is the subject of the finite verb of speaking or commissioning. The action commanded is in the infinitive with the servant as agent.

    3. We follow the *NJV* suggestion in a footnote that MT *gôy* be repointed to *gĕwîyâ*, "body."

For he who has compassion leads them,
    by springs of water he will guide them.
[11]I will make all the mountains into a road,
    my highways will be built up.
[12]These people are coming from a far distance,
    they are coming from the north and from the south,
    they are coming from Syene.[4]
[13]Break into shouts, O heavens,
    cry out with joy, O earth.
    Let the mountains burst forth with exultant cries.
For Yahweh has consoled[5] his people,
    has had mercy on his afflicted ones.

[14]But Zion said,
    "Yahweh has abandoned me,
    my Lord has forgotten me!"
[15]Can a woman forget her nursing infant,
    so as to have no compassion on the child of her womb?
Even if they would forget,
    I would not forget you.
[16]I have you engraved here on my hands,
    your walls are continually before me.[6]
[17]Your children come swiftly,
    those who devastated, razed you, are departing from you.
[18]Look all about you and see,
    they all are assembling, are coming to you.
As I live—oracle of Yahweh—
    you shall don them like jewels,
    deck yourself like a bride.
[19]As for the ruins and rubble of yours,
    the devastated land of yours—

---

4. Syene is a town, in the south of Egypt, near modern Aswan. The phrase "from Migdal to Syene" was proverbial for the whole of Egypt.
5. The word is *niham,* the same word as "Console my people" in 40:1.
6. The walls of a city symbolized the city, as in Psalm 48.

now you will be too crowded for settlers;
    those who devoured you will be far away.
²⁰The children you thought you had lost,
    will yet say in your ears,
"I don't have enough room;
    make room for me to live in."
²¹You will say to yourself,
    "Who bore me these?
I was bereaved and barren,
    exiled and disdained,
    but these—who reared them?
Here I was, left completely alone,
    and these—where are they from?"
²²Thus says the Lord Yahweh,
I am now raising my hand to the nations,
    to the peoples I am raising my banner.
They will bring your children in their arms,
    your daughters will be carried on their shoulders.
²³Kings will tend your children,
    their queens will serve as nurses.
With faces to the ground they will bow to you,
    they shall lick the dust of your feet.
You shall know that it is I, Yahweh;
    none is shamed who waits for me.

²⁴Can spoil be taken from the warrior,
    can captives escape from the victor?
²⁵Thus says Yahweh,
Yes, captives can be taken from the warrior,
    spoil be recovered from the tyrant.
With those who contend with you, I will contend,
    your children I will rescue.
²⁶I will make your persecutors eat their own flesh,
    they shall be drunk with their own blood as with wine.
All flesh will know that I Yahweh give you victory,
    your Redeemer is the Mighty One of Jacob.

COMMENTARY

If chapter 48 was an internal memorandum to Israel warning against preconceptions about the new creation, then chapter 49 is a press release to all the nations (v. lab). It makes public the details of Israel's vocation and of Zion's reward. The prophet has dealt with Israel's vocation before, in the trial scenes of 41:1–42:9, 43:9–44:5 and 44:6–23. Israel was publicly declared, before all nations and all gods, to have a special relation to the sole God. Its special relationship is expressed actively, by the task it is called to perform. Language used of specially called individuals or "servants" in pre-exilic times is now applied to the whole people.

The servant's role was generally defined most clearly in the narratives of their commission. Since the servant's vocation in Second Isaiah is to lead Israel to a new Exodus-Conquest, it is not surprising that his call is modeled on the commission of Moses in Exod 3:1–4:17. The same type of narrative is found also in the commissions of Gideon in Jdg 6:11–24 and especially in that of Jeremiah in Jer 1:4–10. In this type of call Yahweh speaks to the person and appoints him to a task; the person resists the call, pointing to some disability. Moses cites the people's lack of confidence in him (Exod 4:1) and his ineloquence (4:10). Gideon appeals to his own and his clan's low social standing (Jdg 6:15). Jeremiah points to his youth and ineloquence (Jer 1:6). Further conversation, and sometimes signs, are necessary to overcome the person's resistance and send him to his task. In our text, the discouraged servant must be persuaded by extended conversation to go to the task, as is shown by the repeated verbs, "he said," "but I said," "and he said."

The call narrative is not the only traditional item in the chapter. The procession of the people as a flock to the land in vv. 9–11 is known from Exod 15:13–17 and Ps 78:52–55. Zion as a woman bereft of children to whom her Lord brings her children is a scene re-

---

7. Walther Zimmerli in an influential analysis has distinguished between two basic types of call, those like Moses, Gideon and Jeremiah, and those like Isaiah 6 and 1 Kgs 22:19–22, *Ezekiel 1* (Hermeneia; Philadelphia: Fortress, 1979) 97–100.

peated more than once in Jeremiah, especially in chapters 30–31.[8] The picture of Yahweh raising a hand and a banner to the nations as a signal to bring back his children is familiar from Isa 11:10–12. V. 24, a proverb of ineluctable fate, is of the type found in Jer 13:23: "Can the Ethiopian change his skin, or the leopard his spots?"

How is the variety of material unified into a single statement? The major unifying device is parallelism of sections vv. 1–13 with 55 cola and vv. 14–26 with 52 cola. In the first, the resistance of the servant must be overcome; in the second, the disbelief of Zion. The address to Zion in v. 14 would be impossibly abrupt without vv. 1–13. Smaller sections are unified by various means. The dialogue of commission in vv. 1–6 is modeled on a single prototype, as already suggested. V. 8 alludes to v. 6 in its use of the verb "to establish," *hēqîm.* The colon, "I made you a covenant to the peoples," in v. 8 finds its mate in v. 6, "I made you a light to the nations"; the two phrases are elsewhere paired in a similar context (42:6). The picture of children streaming back to a restored Zion in vv. 14–21 is found in earlier texts, e.g. Jer 31:15–22, and in later ones, e.g. Isaiah 60.

Analysis of details supports the case for unity. Though the figure of Moses is the most decisive model for the servant here, the text of Jeremiah (itself modeled on Moses' call) is the immediate model for vv. 1–6. Resistance is overcome through dialogue. The verbs of conversation are underlined in the Jeremiah text. "Before I fashioned you in the womb, I knew you, / a prophet for the nations I appointed you."/ *But I said,* 'Ah, my Lord, Yahweh, I do not know how to speak, I am only a youth.'/ *And Yahweh said to me,* 'Do not say, "I am only a youth," for to all to whom I send you you shall go, all I command you shall speak.' . . . Then Yahweh put forth his hand and touched my mouth; and *Yahweh said to me,* 'I have now put my words in your mouth. See I have set you this day over nations, and kingdoms . . . ' " (Jer 1:4–10). The prophet who is called to be the servant of Yahweh (an intimate and honorable position) pleads his

8. For a balanced discussion of this passage and others in Jeremiah in their relation to Second Isaiah, see Shalom Paul, "Literary and Ideological Echoes of Jeremiah in Deutero-Isaiah," *Proceedings of the Fifth World Congress of Jewish Studies* (Jerusalem: World Union of Jewish Studies, 1971) 102–20.

exhausted and depleted condition[9] as an excuse, yet with an expression of trust tempering the bleakness, v. 4cd.[10] Yahweh denies that the servant's exhaustion disqualifies him to be a servant; the choice was made at birth and is unalterable. In the initial encounter in vv. 1c–3, Yahweh bestows speaking ability, protection and the title of servant. In v. 5cd the people over whom the servant has charge is designated—Israel which is to be guided back to its land. The task of guiding back, of reassembling, is a task that could only be performed for an exiled population. The affirmation of the called one in his office as servant is expanded in v. 5ef. The servant is honored, or affirmed, and the strength of his God has overcome his exhaustion resulting from pointless labor, v. 4ab. So great in fact is the honor of the servant and still more of his master that an exclusively inner-Israel activity is beneath his dignity as minister of the Lord of the world (v. 6de). His work will make him a light to the nations, will make the victory of Yahweh visible to the entire world. "Victory" means that conquest of the desert which makes it a way for Israel to march to Zion.

The scene extends to v. 12 but we must interrupt our exposition to discuss the problem of the identity of the servant arising from this passage. If Israel is the servant according to the text in v. 3b, how could Israel have a mission to Jacob and Israel? One common solution to the problem is to excise the word "Israel" from v. 3b[11] and then to interpret the servant in the passage as an individual. The excision is not text-critically warranted and is unnecessary. The proper answer to the question how servant Israel can have a mission to Israel is to recall that servants in Israel were understood dialectally, in relation to the people to whom they were sent; people and servant were profoundly orientated to each other. Yahweh's servant is not conceivable apart from the people, nor the people without a servant

9. See note 1.

10. Form critics such as Joachim Begrich have argued, largely on the basis of this expression of trust which resembles similar expressions in psalmists' recollection of past distress, e.g. Ps 31:22; Ps 66:18 and Jonah 2:5, that 49:1–6 belongs to the genre of thanksgiving. See his *Studien zur Deuterojesaja* (Munich: Kaiser, 1969, reprint of 1938 edition) 55. Such references to thanksgiving psalms are unnecessary. The type of prophetic call which has shaped the passage sufficiently accounts for the feature.

11. For a full discussion, see Norbert Lohfink, " 'Israel' in Jes 49:3," in *Wort, Leid und Gottesspruch* (Ziegler Volume; ed. J. Schreiner; Forschung zur Bibel 2; Würzburg: Echter Verlag, 1972) 217–229.

standing over against them. Further, the servant often underwent in advance of the people the crisis they were later to undergo so that he could lead them through it. The anticipatory experience of the servant is particularly visible in the two servants whose commission is alluded to in our passage, Moses and Jeremiah. Moses fled Egypt before the wrath of Pharaoh and met Yahweh at Sinai before the people went through the identical process. Jeremiah's personal anguish, especially discernible in his famous laments,[12] foreshadows the popular anguish of the Exile. The servant is what all Israel is called to become. Like Moses, the people are to escape Pharaoh's domain in Egypt to worship in Yahweh's domain in Sinai. Like Jeremiah, they are submissively to undergo the punishment of Exile. The servant is therefore Israel obedient to the divine word. The servant can of course be an individual but all Israel is called to obey the word through him, and the concept can include those Israelites who are associated with the servant in obedience to the present task. In this passage, servant Israel (the prophet and his followers), who is called to display Yahweh's glory on earth (v. 3), has pleaded his exhaustion as an excuse, yet without yielding entirely to despair (v. 4). He is now sent to the people, the *rabbîm,* in such a way as to bring the notice of Yahweh's victory to them.

Having sketched our own solution to the servant question, we return to the second half of vv. 1-12. Vv. 1-6 were an autobiographical account of his commission to servanthood told to the nations, v. 1ab. V. 7 is addressed to Israel, summarizing the rise from humiliation to public honor. The entire verse makes explicit why Israel is a light to the nations (v. 6). Its return to its own land means that its subjection to Babylon is ended ("servant of rulers," v. 7d); kings of the world have to recognize a power superior to Babylon's.

Vv. 8-12 specify the task given the servant in vv. 1-6. Rescued from the exhaustion about which he complained (v. 4), like the typical poor person of the psalms,[13] he is able to rescue and restore the survivors of Israel. The task of Moses is again evoked as it had been in vv. 1-6 to describe the servant's leading in the desert (vv. 9-11)

---

12. Jer 11:18-12:6; 15:10-21; 17:14-18; 18:18-23; 20:7-13; 20:14-18.
13. A good parallel is Ps 69:13, "But as for me, my prayer is to thee, Yahweh. / At a time of favor, O God, / in the abundance of thy steadfast love respond to me, / in your sure victory."

and allotment of the land (v. 8ef). The text attributes the whole Exodus-Conquest to Moses with support from some texts.[14] As already
suggested, "I fashioned you and made you a covenant to the nations"
(v. 8d), parallels the phrase "light to the nations" from earlier in the
speech, in v. 6d. There are other links between vv. 8–12 and 1–6: repeated vocabulary, syntax[15] and ideas. The commission to restore Israel means reallotting their heritages in the land (v. 8ef), for without
their lands the tribes would hardly consider themselves restored. The
actual return begins with an address to prisoners and those in darkness, v. 9. As was the case in the similar detailing of the servant's
task in 42:6–7, the exiles are considered to be under the power of primordial darkness. They are to come forth and be shepherded by
Yahweh. The picture of Israel led home as a flock is known from
Exod 15:13–17, Ps 78:52–55 and in Isa 40:10–11. The crowds stream
homeward from all the world. In v. 13 the elements of the world rejoice, as they do in 44:23 and 45:8.

The gathering of the exiles is only half the story. As in the poem
in Jer 31:15–22, the bereft mother must be consoled, vv. 14–26. The
feelings of Mother Zion are too complex and profound to be instan-
taneously converted to the uninhibited joy just shown by inanimate
nature. Gently and gradually the mother is reassured. She is allowed
her incredulous questions. Her reluctance is undone by the same divine conversation that healed the servant in vv. 1–6. Zion expresses
in vv. 14 and 24 fatalistic sentiments in proverbs which had penetrat-
ed into the people's marrow. She cites grim popular sayings instanced also in other exilic literature: "The fathers have eaten sour
grapes and the children's teeth are set on edge" (Ezek 18:2); "Our
bones are dried up, and our hope is lost; we are clean cut off" (Ezek
37:11);[16] "My situation is hid from Yahweh; my case escapes the notice of Yahweh" (40:27). Proverbs were more than slogans. They
were statements of the laws of an unchanging universe which man
could not change but only record and conform to. Yahweh's over-
turning of them here is a striking instance of his ability to do a new
thing.

---

14. Moses leads in holy war and distributes the land (of Transjordan) in Deuteronomy 1–3.
15. On syntax, see note 2.
16. Cf. also Ezek 18:25.

The section requires little comment. To Zion's complaint that Yahweh has forgotten her, Yahweh proclaims his maternal instinct toward his child. In v. 16, he adapts the well-known metaphor of constant remembrance, "And you shall bind them [the words of the Law] as a sign upon your hand, and they shall be as frontlets between your eyes" (Deut 6:8), to console Israel.

In vv. 17–21 the ruins of Zion are rebuilt as the children return, the repair of the buildings reflecting the soothing of the bereavement. The glory of a city is its splendid buildings and thronging crowds. As the children approach (vv. 17–18), Yahweh swears to the mother that these children will adorn the city now abuilding (vv. 18–19). She cries out with slowly awakening delight (v. 21). The reader cannot but think of Lady Babylon who has been made to strip off her adornments and, shamefully exposed, leave the ruined city for exilic distress.

As the nations came to recognize the hand of Yahweh in the exaltation of their onetime vassal (v. 7), they similarly react to the restoration of the city (v. 23). The divine hand is raised (in an allusion to 11:10–11) and the nations, represented by their kings, carry the children. Israel will recognize in the event that Yahweh never disappoints those who wait for him.

The last word to the mother is the destruction of all proverbs that deny Yahweh's control of history, that attribute control of history to the might of empires (v. 24). The prisoners will be brought home because of the divine decision to contend with those who contend with Israel. The gruesome fate of Israel's former persecutors, to eat their own flesh and drink their own blood, is a conventional curse of covenant violation in the ancient Near East. It alludes to cannibalism in siege-induced famine.[17] As Zion recognized Yahweh as the one who does not disappoint his faithful, so "all flesh" will recognize that Israel's savior and avenger is Yahweh.

In this long passage the servant informs the nations how his call now affects them. The nations will see in the return of a scattered people and in the revival of the devastated city the evidence of Yahweh's unique power.

---

17. See Lev 26:29 and Deut 28:53–57.

13th Speech

THE LIGHT THAT FOLLOWS
PUNISHING DARKNESS

[50:1–51:8]

¹Thus says Yahweh,
Where is the document of divorce for your mother¹
    by which I sent her away?
To which of my creditors
    did I sell you?
For your sins were you sold
    for your rebellions was your mother dismissed.
²Why, when I came, was no one there,
    when I called, did no one answer?²
Is my hand too weak to rescue?
    Do I not have the power to liberate?
By my (mere) rebuke I dried up Sea,

---

1. V. 1 speaks of the disruption of relationships between Yahweh and Zion and between Zion and her children, a double loss described already in the case of Babylon in 47:8–9 and Zion in 49:14–26. The Hebrew makes the questions and answers extremely clear by the use of the interjection *hēn* to point out the answers. The interjection appears also in answers in 40:15 and 44:11. Hence "For your sins were you sold . . ." is the answer to the first question and "By my mere rebuke I dried up Sea . . ." is the answer to the second question.

2. In the light of the addresses to Zion in 51:1–8 in the latter part of this speech, Yahweh's coming must be his coming to his city Zion. The calling and answering in v. 2b refers to sacral transactions in that holy spot. Ezekiel 43:1–5 speaks of Yahweh's coming to his Temple.

I made Rivers desert.[3]
Its fish stank for lack of water,
    they lay dead on the dry ground.[4]
[3]I clothed the heavens in blackness,
    I made sackcloth its covering.

[4]The Lord Yahweh gave me the tongue of the disciples,
    to know how to speak with the faint in the time.[5]
He roused me each morning,
    he roused my ear,
    to listen like the disciples.
[5]The Lord Yahweh opened my ear,
    I did not rebel,
    I did not run away.
[6]I offered my back to the smiters,
    my cheek to those who plucked out my beard.
I did not hide my face
    from shame and spittle.
[7]The Lord Yahweh offers me help,
    therefore I am not shamed.
Therefore I have made my face like flint,
    I know that I will not be ashamed.
[8]Near is the one who declares me innocent.
    Who will contend with me?
    Let us stand up together.
Who is my adversary?
    Let him approach me.
[9]The Lord Yahweh gives me aid.
    Who is he that will find me guilty?

---

3. The imperfect tenses of the verbs in vv. 2e–3 seem to imitate the archaic preterite of the old cosmogonies.

4. Correcting MT *ṣāmā'* "thirst" to *ṣāmē'* "dry ground" as in 44:3, with *NJV*.

5. *Limmudîm* "disciples," occurs only here and in 8:16 within the Book. The text is corrupt. We read *lā 'ēt*, with the old Greek, and assume that the author is alluding to 9:1 (Heb 8:23) *kā'ēt hāri'šôn* and *wĕhā'ahărôn*, "in the former time" and "the latter (time)." The syntax of divine commission is similar to that already noted in 42:6–7; 44:24–28; 49:5, 8–9: *Yhwh nātan lî . . . lāda'at . . . 'et yā'ēp dabbēr* [MT *dābār*] i.e. finite verb of commission followed by infinitives expressing the commissioned one's duties.

All of them like a garment will wear out,
the moth shall consume them.
[10]Who of you fears Yahweh,
listens to the voice of his servant,
who has walked in darkness,
is without light?
(Who) trusts in the name of Yahweh,
relies on his God?
[11]All of you who kindle fire,[6]
who light firebrands,
walk in the light of your fire,
of the firebrands you have lit.
From my hand has this come upon you,
in the place you lie.

[51:1] Listen to me, you who pursue righteousness ($ṣdq$),
who seek after Yahweh.
Look to the rock from which you were hewn,
the quarry you were dug from.
[2]Look to Abraham your father,
to Sarah who bore you.
Though (only) one when I called him,
I blessed him, I made him many.
[3]For Yahweh comforts Zion,
he comforts all her ruins.
He will make her desert like Eden,
her aridity like the Garden of Yahweh.
Rejoicing and joy will be found in her,
thanksgiving and the sound of music.

[4]Attend to me, O my people,
O my people, give ear to me.

---

6. The verses are very obscure. In the light of our understanding of the verses as
the positive exhortation of the rescued just man to his hearers, we take them in a positive sense. The passage in Isa 2:1–4 which is explicitly referred to in 51:4 concludes:
"O house of Jacob, come let us walk in the light of Yahweh" (Isa 2:5). The bed of pain
is the symbol of Exile. Our understanding is of course tentative, but it does have the
merit of making an easy transition to 51:1.

For torah goes forth from me,
  my decision for a light to the nations.
In a moment I will bring it;
  ⁵near is my victory,
my salvation goes forth,
  my arms rule over the peoples.
For me the coastlands hope,
  for my arm they wait.

⁶Lift your eyes to the heavens,
  look to the earth below.
Though the heavens will dissipate like smoke,
  earth like a garment will wear out;
  its inhabitants like gnats will die,
yet my salvation will be forever,
  my victory remain unbroken.

⁷Listen to me, you who know righteousness (*ṣdq*),
  people who have the torah already in your minds.
Do not fear the contempt of men,
  at their revilings do not be dismayed.
⁸For the moth will consume them like a garment,
  the worm will eat them up like wool.
But my victory will be forever,
  my salvation for ages upon ages.

COMMENTARY

This section reminds us that Second Isaiah has left us not a logical treatise but supple speeches shaped by the realities of confused exilic life. Most of its themes—Yahweh's return to his bride Zion (50:1–2), the vindication of the humiliated servant (50:4–9), the glorification of Zion (51:1–8)—have been seen before. But the shaping of the themes is fresh and makes an appeal that is different from other speeches where one or another of the themes may appear.

First we must demonstrate that the section is a single poem. Some phrases are repeated with only slight variation in different sections, suggesting deliberate reprise: "near is the one who declares me innocent (*qārôb maṣdîqî*, 50:8)," "near is my victory (*qārôb ṣidqî*, 51:5)." Repetition of the metaphor "to be worn out like a garment" is found in 50:9cd, 51:6cde and 8ab. Nearly all commentators deny that 50:4–11 have anything to do with the immediately following 51:1–8[7] despite the repetitions noted. The best proof for unity comes from the single train of thought.[8]

Yahweh's dismissal of his wife and children was only temporary, due to his own decision to punish sin, 50:1–2d. It could not have been due to his enemies' superior force since he defeated them in the act of creation (50:2e–3). The servant with the insight of a true disciple understood the true cause and purpose of exilic pain. He reckoned it as punishment and faithfully bore it (50:4–11). The presence of Yahweh which vindicated the disciple in the chaos of exile is now to be found in the holy city of Zion, the one sure point in the universe where Yahweh's victory can be experienced (51:1–8).

In the first section, 50:1–3, Yahweh denies that his new relationship to his people can be understood on the basis of legal custom—the law regulating divorce[9] and the law regulating a person's selling of his children to creditors.[10] No document of divorce exists for God and his people. He has no creditors. The twofold deprivation of husband and children has been seen before in chapters 47 and 49. Israel suffered deprivation for her sins, and not because some external agency compelled Yahweh to act. He has in fact shown his mastery over the most powerful forces in human experiences—Sea and the heavenly bodies whose light regulates human existence. In the one case he dried up Sea's waters, and in the other he shut off the light given off by sun, moon and stars, by throwing sackcloth over them (50:2e–3).

The speaker in 50:4–11 shifts abruptly from divine to human as the disciple describes how he faithfully and willingly endured great

---

7. Muilenburg is one of the few. Bonnard, *Le Second Isaïe*, p. 237, notes some affinities between chapter 50 and 51:1–8 but concludes that the differences are greater than the similarities.

8. The end of the poem seems easy to prove. Isa 52:9, with its address to the arm of Yahweh, narrates the battle between Yahweh and the Sea in a version different from that of 50:2–3.

9. Deut 24:1–4 and cf. Jer 3:1–5.

10. Exod 21:7–11; and 2 Kgs 4:1.

suffering. He was taught the true meaning of the divine punishment. He knew his vindicator was near and that he would not be publicly shamed (50:4–9). At the end of his story of rescue he turns to the circle of his hearers and tells them that they may enjoy the same divine protection (50:10–11). The entire section seems modeled on the thanksgiving psalm, a common genre in the Psalter. Such psalms are essentially reports of divine rescue from distress. They often describe the distress in heightened terms, the psalmist recalling his near despair in order to affirm publicly that Yahweh has saved him. Not infrequently the rescued psalmist turns to his audience and assures them that the rescue he has just narrated can be shared in by all who desire life, pursue justice, etc. Psalm 34 is a good example from which to draw some verses for comparison with Second Isaiah's adaptation. "I sought Yahweh and he answered me. . . . Come, O sons, listen to me and I will teach you the fear of Yahweh. What man is there who desires life, / and covets many days, that he may enjoy good? Keep your tongue from evil, and your lips from speaking deceit" (Ps 34:4, 11–13).

Comparison with the thanksgiving psalm is instructive but the section still requires detailed examination of its own structure. The text of v. 4 is uncertain but the meaning is clear: Yahweh has given the speaker the tongue of a disciple to know how to speak with the faint (yā‘ēp). The "faint" have been met before in Second Isaiah; they are the ones who have not learned how to draw strength from their God (40:28–31). They are like the circle of hearers who are instructed by the thanksgiving of the psalmist.

Though vv. 4–9 are commonly called the third servant song, the speaker here is not called a servant but a disciple. This title holds the key to the passage. The term seems to come from two texts on the disciples of First Isaiah, 8:16–18 with borrowings of vocabulary from the surrounding verses 8:19–9:7 and 30:8–14. The eighth century prophet, frustrated by the people's unwillingness to listen to his message that God was about to punish Judah, wrote it on a scroll which he sealed and left with his disciples.[11] When judgment fell, the written message was there with his disciples who would know the mean-

---

11. Disciples, *limmûdîm*, occurs only in 8:16 and 50:4. Second Isaiah uses the plural as does First Isaiah, perhaps alluding to a circle of disciples of which he is one.

ing of the punishment and how to respond to it. Isaiah 8 predicts the judgment will be deep darkness and distress (8:22) but will be followed by a time of great light (9:1–2). "And they look to the earth and behold distress and darkness, the gloom of anguish; and they will be thrust into thick darkness. But there will be no gloom for her that was in anguish. In the former time (*ʿēt*) he humbled the land of Zebulon and the land of Naphtali but in the latter time he will make glorious the way of the sea, the land beyond the Jordan, Galilee of the nations. (The people who walked in darkness have seen a great light; those who dwelt in a land of deep darkness, on them has light shined." The conceptual and verbal resemblances between the texts of First and Second Isaiah strongly suggest that Second Isaiah sees the end of the exile as the turning point from darkness to light predicted by the old prophet. Now it is time for the disciples to speak out the testimony, the true understanding of divine punishment and of salvation. The word of the disciple is for the faint, those whose spirit was broken by the first step of the two-step pedagogy of darkness and light described by the First Isaiah.

The second Isaian passage regarding disciples, 30:8–15, has also made its contribution. Its vocabulary is repeated in 50:4–11 in a striking way.[12] Because the people were rebellious, would not hear the teaching, and trusted in oppression, First Isaiah wrote his message down so that the written record could convict the people later when judgment struck. The disciple in the Deutero-Isaian passage has shown himself to be just the opposite of the people; he is not rebellious but is alert to the teaching, trusting in Yahweh and relying on his God. He has trustfully submitted to the divine punishment. Like the classic sufferer of exilic deprivation portrayed in Lamentations 3:25, 28, 30, he waits for Yahweh. "Let him sit alone in silence / when he has it laid on him . . . let him give his cheek to the smiter, / and be filled with insults." Amid the convulsions of the Exile the disciple has felt the presence of God. To express that reassuring pres-

---

12.   *Isa 50:4–11*
lišmôaʿ kallimmûdîm (v. 4e)
ʾānôkî lōʾ mārîtî (v. 5b)
yibṭaḥ bĕšēm YHWH (v. 10e)

wĕyiššāʿēn bēʾlōhāyw (v. 10f)

Isa 30:18–14
bānîm lōʾ ʾābû šĕmôʿ tôrat YHWH (v. 9)
ʿam mĕrî hûʾ (v. 9)
wattibṭĕḥû bĕʿōšeq wĕnālōz (v. 12)
wattiššāʿănû ʿālāyw (v. 12)

ence, he makes use of concepts from the Psalms of Zion. "God is in her midst, she shall not be moved; / God will help her before morning. / The nations rage, the kingdoms totter; / he utters his voice, the earth melts" (Ps 46:5–6 *RSV*). The prophet's discovery of the presence of God in the turbulence of exile will have important implications for 51:1–8.

The disciple, then, has revealed "in the latter time" the true meaning of the exilic darkness that all have been suffering. It has been sent by Yahweh to punish Israel for its sins. Disciples of Yahweh knew the divine purpose in the afflictions and so accepted it as chastening and as destined to end with the return of Yahweh to his people. The divine presence that sustained the disciples is now to be found in the holy city. This is the theme of the four stanzas of chapter 51, each introduced by the masculine plural imperative, employed when an address to all Israel is made: 51:1–3, 4–5, 6, 7–8.

The first stanza, 51:1–3, is addressed to those who "pursue righteousness" (v. 1a), i.e. the vindication which the disciple declares he has already experienced. The first verse seems to allude to the advice given by the vindicated disciple in 50:10 and to expand it. Those who seek what the disciple offers are to look at the source from which they sprung, Abraham and Sarah. When only a single couple, Yahweh blessed them and made their descendants many. The mention of Sarah is unusual and provides a clue to the sudden mention of Zion in v. 3. Abraham and Sarah were "one," i.e. alone, childless until Sarah's barrenness was healed by Yahweh. Yahweh has now consoled Zion as a husband.[13] The desert of her sterility has been healed. Joyous song fills the city which was once silent ruins. Zion is the place to find the righteousness that comes from nearness to God.

V. 6 imitates the psalmic Zion songs which declare the holy city to be the central and firm point of a universe that is tottering. See Psalms 46 and 48. The next stanza, vv. 7–8, addresses those who already experience righteousness, who already have the torah in their minds. It is for those who have actually come to Zion and have heard the torah that has gone forth. The verses counsel the people in Zion

---

13. The verb "console" (*nhm*) is used in a sexual sense in 2 Sam 12:24. "Then David comforted his wife, Bathsheba, and went in to her, and lay with her; and she bore a son, and he called his name Solomon." (*RSV*)

not to fear human contempt. The moth will consume those who taunt them, like a garment. It is the same phrase used of the disciple's enemies (50:9cd), underscoring again that the divine presence that sustained the disciple in the Exile is to be found in Zion.

The speech as a whole declares that the disciples, i.e. those who consider themselves disciples of First Isaiah, especially in his teaching on punishment and restoration, speak the truth regarding the vindicating presence of Yahweh. They have offered their back to the smiter, i.e. have accepted the Exile as heaven-sent and been rescued. The teaching of First Isaiah that light follows darkness can now be proclaimed. Those of their fellow Israelites who wish to find the presence of Yahweh will find it in Zion, now brought back from its ruins to be a source of salvation for all. Analogies based on traditional law on divorce or on debts that say Yahweh's relationship to his people has ended are completely wrong. No tradition can stay his love which justifies the people.

14th Speech

A PRAYER THAT YAHWEH DESTROY THE FOE AND BRING HIS PEOPLE TO ZION

[51:9–52:12]

⁹Awake, awake, clothe yourself with might,
    arm of Yahweh.
Awake as in days of old,
    generations long ago.
Was it not you who hacked Rahab[1] in pieces,
    pierced Dragon through?
¹⁰Was it not you who dried up Sea,
    the waters of Great Deep,
who made the depths of Sea a way
    that the redeemed might cross?
¹¹Let those liberated by Yahweh return,
    let them come to Zion singing.
Let everlasting joy crown their needs,
    let them obtain gladness and joy.
Let sorrow and mourning flee.[2]

¹²I, I am the one who comforts you.

---

1. Rahab, Dragon, Sea, and Great Deep are all allies of the monster Sea, or perhaps epithets of the same monster.
2. With most commentators we translate the verbs as future, and hence part of the prayer for future restoration, although some take them as past, determined by the "of old" of v. 9c.

Who are you to fear man who dies,
    a mere human who fares like grass,
[13]and forget Yahweh who made you,
        who stretches out the heavens,
        who sets the earth on its foundations?
    (Who are you) to remain in terror every moment of the day
        before the wrath of the oppressor
        as he aims to cut you down.
    Where is the wrath of the oppressor?
[14]Quickly the one bowed down[3] will be freed,
        he will not descend in death to the Pit,
        he will not lack food.
[15]I am Yahweh your God
        who touch the sea and its waves roar;
        Yahweh of hosts is my name.
[16]I have put my words in your mouth,
        in the shadow of my hand I have given you shelter.
    I, who stretch out the heavens, who set the earth on its
            foundations,
        who say to Zion, "You are my people!"

[17]Rouse yourself, rouse yourself,
        stand up, Jerusalem!
    You who have drunk from the hand of Yahweh
        the cup of his wrath;
    have drained to the dregs
        the bowl, the cup of staggering.
[18]There is none to lead her home
        from all the sons she has borne.
    There is none to take her by the hand
        from the sons she has reared.
[19]These two things have befallen you:
        wrack and ruin—who consoles you?

---

3. As 52:2c makes clear by its use of *hitpattĕhiw,* the meaning is bent down with chains, presumably from the oppressor.

Famine and sword—who comforts you?[4]
20Your children lie in a swoon
   at the corner of every street,
   like an antelope caught in a net,
filled with the wrath of Yahweh,
   the rebuke of your God.

21Therefore hear this, afflicted one,
   you who are drunk but not with wine.
22Thus says your Lord Yahweh,
   your God who champions his people.
I have now taken from your hand
   the cup of staggering;
the bowl, the cup of my wrath,
   you shall never drink again.
23I have put it in the hand of your tormentors,
   those who have said to you,
"Get down that we may walk over you.
   Put your back on the ground,
   be like the street for people to walk on."

52:1 Awake, awake, clothe yourself
   with your might, O Zion!
Clothe yourself with glorious garments,
   O Jerusalem, holy city.
For never again shall there come to you
   the uncircumcised and the unclean.
2Arise, shake off the dust,
   sit (on your throne), O Jerusalem!
Be freed of the chains upon your neck,
   captive fair Zion.
3[For thus says Yahweh,
Without any payment were you sold,
   not for money will you be redeemed.

---

4. We read yĕnaḥămēk for MT 'ănḥămēk.

⁴'For thus says the Lord Yahweh,
 To Egypt my people went down at the first to sojourn there,
  but Assyria for nothing oppressed him.
 ⁵But now what am I doing here—oracle of Yahweh—
  for my people are taken away without any payment.
 Their rulers howl—oracle of Yahweh—
  continually all the day long my name is profaned.
 ⁶Surely my people will recognize my name,
  surely, in that day, that I am the one who speaks "Here I
   am!"]

⁷How welcome upon the mountains
  are the feet of the herald,
 announcing peace,
   reporting good news,
 announcing victory,
   saying to Zion,
   "Your God reigns!"
 ⁸Hark, your watchmen lift up their voices,
  together they raise a jubilant shout.
 Every eye shall indeed look upon
  the return of Yahweh to Zion.

⁹Break forth into singing,
   ruins of Jerusalem.
 For Yahweh has consoled his people,
  has redeemed Jerusalem.
 ¹⁰Yahweh has bared his holy arm
  in the sight of all the nations.
 All the ends of the earth have seen
  the victory of our God.
 ¹¹Turn away, turn away, get out of there,
  touch nothing unclean.
 Go out from her midst, keep yourself pure,
  you who carry the vessels of Yahweh.
 ¹²Do not go forth in haste,
   do not march forth in flight.

For Yahweh walks before you,
the God of Israel is your rear-guard.

COMMENTARY

The section we propose to be a single speech may strike the
reader as a baroque assemblage of fragments. Only when the verses
are read as deliberately evocative of the lament liturgy celebrated in
the old Temple when mortal danger threatened the entire community does its unity appear.

In the genre of national lament, the people prayed to the God
who had brought them into being not to allow their enemies to anni-
hilate them. Israel was brought into being by the Exodus-Conquest;
hence that deed is recalled in the prayer. The laments retell or "remember" in a liturgical sense the Exodus-Conquest—sometimes only
allusively—in order to put God on the spot. Is he the kind of God
who will let some other power wipe out his handiwork? In Psalms
44, 74, 77, 89, examples of national laments, one finds three elements. The first is the allusion to the creative moment for Israel, the
Exodus-Conquest: "I will recite the deeds of Yahweh, I will recite
your act of old. . . . Your way was through the sea, / your path was
through the great waters. / You led your people like a flock."[5] The
second element is a vivid description of the affliction which seems to
belie Yahweh's action: "Your enemies have roared in the midst of
your Temple, / they have set up their own signs as signs."[6] Third,
there is the plea for immediate divine intervention: "Rouse yourself!
Why do you sleep, Lord? / Awake, do not cast us off forever."[7]
There is a fourth element, not generally preserved, which is of great
importance for understanding the divine-human encounter of the
psalms: the oracle in response. Generally the laments of the Psalter
do not preserve it (Psalm 60 is an exception) because it is the priest's
part rather than the community's. Second Isaiah, as we have seen al-

---

5. Ps 77:11, 19–20.
6. Ps 74:4.
7. Ps 44:23.

ready, borrowed extensively from the Psalter. All four elements of
the national lament show up in our passage, adapted of course to
preaching purposes. The allusion to the Exodus-Conquest is in 51:9–
11. The plea for divine intervention is found in 51:9, "Awake as in
days of old," and echoed in 51:10, 51:17 and 52:1. The recital of the
deeds of old is in 51:9e–11. The vivid depiction of the afflictions is, in
a masterly shift, put in the mouth of Yahweh who thereby shows he
needs no reminding of the sufferings of his beloved Zion (51:17–20).
The fourth component, the divine response, has served as model for
the rebuking consolation to the people in 51:12–16 and the more
tender address to Zion in 51:21–52:2.

A single genre has shaped 51:9–52:2, implying the unity of at
least these verses. Cross-references within the poem furnish addition-
al evidence of conscious design. Within the complaint-recital of
51:9–11 and the divine response in 51:12–16, the double question of
vv. 9–10 "Was it not you . . ." is taken up in the extended "who are
you . . ." in vv. 12–13. The mastery over Sea in vv. 9–10 is echoed in
v. 15. The call to Yahweh to awake (*'ûrî*) in 51:9 is picked up and
applied to Jerusalem in v. 17 (*hit'ôrᵉrî*) and in 52:1 (*'ûrî*), hinting
perhaps that Yahweh's might is made available to exhausted Jerusalem.[8] The recital of the return (*šûb*) of the redeemed in 50:11a is fulfilled in the return (*šûb*) of Yahweh in 52:8. The exhortation to
embark on a new Exodus in 52:9–11 is also a reprise of the same text.
What evidence is there that 52:1–2+7–10 is part of the discourse?
To console Zion by telling her, in 51:21–23, that her tormentors will
be forced to drink the same cup of suffering is insufficient consolation since her chief suffering was the absence of her children (51:18–
20). Only the restoration of her children in 52:1–2+7–10 constitutes
suitable consolation.

The main points of the speech should be clear from the above
remarks on genre and unity. Some further remarks remain to be
made on each of the sections. Vv. 9–11 seek to wake the divine warrior[9] by reminding him of his great deeds of old—the defeat of Sea
and the procession of the liberated people to Zion. In short, the

---

8. As in Isa 40:28–31 and 50:4.
9. Cf. Ps 44:23–24; Ps 78:65–66 and Isa 42:13–17.

prayer is that the power of Babylon be broken and that the people return to Zion.

The oracle of salvation in vv. 12–16 responds exactly to the complaint. Yahweh's repeated "I" shows that he is not sleeping, that he is Israel's comforter. "Who are you . . ." (*mî 'att*) in v. 12b, as suggested above, rebukes "was it not you . . ." (*hălô' 'att hî'*) in vv. 9e and 10a, implying that it is rather Israel who sleeps. For the people are in terror of a mere human oppressor (Babylon), forgetting that Yahweh who has created them will free them from their oppressor's power (v. 14). He retains mastery over the sea (v. 15). The close correspondence between complaint-recital and response continues in v. 16. Israel has received Yahweh's protective word about Zion. It is thus an answer to their prayer in vv. 10b–11 to return to Zion.

The reference to Zion in v. 16d leads to the next section on Zion, 51:17–20. The first word "rouse yourself" alludes back to v. 9. As vv. 12–16 implied that Israel, not Yahweh, was asleep and dull, so these verses acknowledge the stupor of Zion and wake her from it. Second Isaiah seems to have drawn the metaphor of the cup of Yahweh's wrath from Jer 25:15–38. Jeremiah there equates the effect of Yahweh's punishing sword with drunkenness. Zion was forced to submit to the Babylonian military might, to drink to the dregs the allotted cup. In her drunken state no one guided her. In a Ugaritic text the ideal son is described, "who takes him [his father] by the hand when he is drunk, / carries him home when he is sated with wine."[10] Not only is the mother Zion dazed by the punishment; she is disgraced in having no children to lead her home. The reversal of her fortunes will not only be the vengeance upon her enemies (vv. 22–23) but, most important, the restoration of her children (52:1–2 + 7–10).

Her restoration is complete only with her arraying herself in garments befitting the beloved of Yahweh, 52:1–2. One immediately thinks of the stripping, exile, and enslavement of Zion's opposite, Queen Babylon, in 47:1–4.

The next verses, 52:3–6, are a series of glosses. They do not use the parallelism otherwise met with in Second Isaiah. "Assyria" for "Chaldea" is unique; "for nothing" (*bĕ'epes*) in v. 5 is an uncharacteristic use of the word. Sentiments from 51:1 are here borrowed for

10. *CTA* (2 Aqht) 17.1.31–32 and 2.5–6. *ANET*, p. 150.

a different context. The verses are not completely clear but seem to say that Yahweh will not permit the profanation of his name by Chaldea's gratuitous spoliation of Israel. He will take action that will show his people he is present to them.

Vv. 7–8 describe the coming of Yahweh from the point of view of the expectant city, in the person of the municipal watchmen who wait tensely for news. Another passage, 2 Sam 18:19–33, similarly builds suspense through the device of watchmen's conversation. The lament has been answered. The powerful arm of Yahweh has redeemed Jerusalem. In this way the divine command that opened the book in 40:1, "comfort my people," becomes actual.

Vv. 11–12 are a coda, urging all to leave Babylon portrayed as a new Egypt through the citation of the rare word used of the old Exodus, "in haste." Exod 12:11 has said "and you shall eat it [the Passover lamb] in haste." No need to fear. Yahweh is about to lead the stately and secure procession back to Zion.

In this entire speech one sees the pastoral plan of the prophet. The people are to believe that their Lord can overcome their oppressors and lead them home to a Jerusalem restored to queenly dignity.

15th Speech

THE MANY CONFESS THAT
YAHWEH UPHOLDS HIS SERVANT

[52:13–53:12]

¹³Behold my servant prevails;
    he is high, lifted up,
    exalted exceedingly.
¹⁴As many were appalled at him—
    so far from human his appearance,
    his features unrecognizable as a man's—
¹⁵So did he startle¹ many nations,
    kings covered their mouths at the sight of him.
For what was not told them they have seen,
    what they never heard they have experienced.

⁵³:¹ Who can believe what we have heard?
    The arm of Yahweh² to whom has it been revealed?
²He grew up before him like a sapling,
    like a root out of dry ground.
No grace, no appeal did he possess to make us look at him,
    no beauty to attract us to him.
³Despised, shunned by people,
    he was a man in pain, familiar with sickness.

---

1. "Startle" is a not wholly satisfactory guess. MT apparently means "to sprin-kle" in purification but this is syntactically difficult.
2. As H. L. Ginsberg suggests in the footnote in *NJV* the meaning is "the vindi-cation the arm of the Lord effects."

As someone who hides his face from us,[3]
despised, we took no account of him.
[4]Surely, our sickness he bore,
our pain he shouldered.
But we accounted him afflicted,
smitten by God and abused.
[5]But he was thrust through for our rebellion,
crushed for our offenses.
The punishment that made us whole was upon him,
by his stripes we are healed.
[6]All of us like sheep had gone astray,
each went his own way.
Yahweh laid on him
the iniquity of us all.

[7]He was oppressed, he was afflicted,
he opened not his mouth.
Like a lamb he was led to slaughter,
like a ewe before her shearers he was dumb,
he opened not his mouth.
[8]By coercive judgment he was taken away,
of his dwelling who can tell?
For he was cut off from the land of the living,
for the sin of his people[4] he was struck down.
[9]They made his grave with the wicked,
his tomb with evildoers,[5]
though he had done no violence,
and there was no wickedness in his mouth.

[10]But Yahweh was pleased[6] to crush him, to afflict him,
when he made himself an offering for sin.

---

3. Again with *NJV* note, the gesture is that of a leper. See Lev 13:45f.

4. Sense suggests that MT *'ammî,* "my people," be read *'ammô,* "his people." *Wāw* and *yôd* are virtually indistinguishable in the Herodian script.

5. MT literally is "and with the rich in his death." The versions support *bāmātô,* "his tomb." For MT *'āšîr, 'ōsê ra',* "workers of evil," is often proposed.

6. In 42:21, the same expression is found, "It pleased Yahweh for his own justice's sake, / that he [the servant] should glorify the Teaching and exalt it." The expression emphasizes the inscrutable purpose of God.

He shall see his offspring, shall lengthen his days,
   the good pleasure of Yahweh shall prosper in his hands.
[11]Out of the anguish of his soul he shall see light,[7]
   he shall be made happy because of his knowledge.
The righteous one, my servant, will make the many
      righteous,
   their offenses he bears.
[12]Therefore I will bestow on him a portion with the many,
   with the mighty he shall share the booty;
because he has exposed his soul to death,
   with sinners he was reckoned.
He has borne the sin of the many,
   he has interceded for their sins.[8]

COMMENTARY

This speech, called since the analysis of Bernhard Duhm the fourth servant song, is the most intriguing and controverted part of Second Isaiah. Does it indeed say that the servant has taken on himself the sins of the nations and justified them before God? Did the servant actually die and rise from the dead? Who is the servant—an historical individual or ideal Israel? These are only some of the questions.

That the passage is a complete discourse is doubted by very few,[9] so definitely is it marked off from what precedes and what follows by its focus on the suffering servant. Narrative in the third person in 53:1–11b is framed by divine speech in the first person ("my servant" in 52:13 and 53:11c) at the beginning, 52:13–15 and the end, 53:11c–12. There is further agreement that the conventions of the thanksgiving psalm have influenced the passage just as they have the third servant song in 50:4–11. The thanksgiving psalm is essentially the psalmist's report of Yahweh's rescue of him from mortal

---

7. MT is to be emended *yir'eh 'ôr* with OG, 1QIsa[ab] and 1QIsa[ab].
8. We emend *pōšĕ'îm* to *piš'ām* implied by OG, 1QIsa[ab].
9. One recent exception is R. N. Whybray, *Thanksgiving for a Liberated Prophet: An Interpretation of Isaiah Chapter 53 (Journal for the Study of the Old Testament Supplement Series 4; Sheffield: Journal for the Study of the Old Testament, 1978) 163, fn. 1.

danger. The danger is often dramatized as attacks upon the innocent just person by sickness, wild beasts, intrigues by former friends, rigged legal proceedings. Yahweh's rescue functions as a judicial verdict for the innocent sufferer, establishing his innocence and the malice of his accusers. He then tells what Yahweh has done for him "in the assembly of the saints," thus glorifying his Lord in the sight of all. The action of our passage resembles that of the typical thanksgiving psalm—rescue from mortal danger as vindication—but with extremely important differences. One major difference is in the speaker. In the Psalms the psalmist speaks throughout. Here Yahweh speaks at the beginning and the end; another voice speaks in the middle section. The servant is totally silent. He "opened not his mouth" as if to dramatize the incapacity of the afflicted righteous person to defend himself.[10] The prophetic preacher adapted the genre with considerable freedom.

Despite the wide measure of agreement on the dimensions and genre of the poem, there is a considerable spectrum of opinion about its meaning. Some of the difficulty arises from its echoes in the New Testament[11] which led to its becoming embroiled in early Jewish-Christian controversy. Dispute naturally centered on the identity of the servant, whether his suffering was vicarious and whether the nations were the speaker in 53:1–11b. Duhm's isolation of the section as one of the four servant songs in his book of 1875 and in his commentary of 1892 maintained the divorce of text from context and its entanglement with the traditional emotion-laden controversies. One result of the isolation of the songs from the rest of Second Isaiah was an almost obsessive interest in identifying the servant with an historical person.[12] Finally, difficulty arises from textual damage in 52:14–15 and 53:10 and from some unusual expressions.

In the first section, 52:13–15, Yahweh tells a broad public that

---

10. See Ps 39:2, 9.
11. See Mark 10:45, 14:24 and parallels where Hebrew *rabbîm* lies behind Greek *polloi;* and Acts 8:28–35.
12. For surveys of opinion on various attempts to identify the servant, see C. R. North, *The Suffering Servant in Deutero-Isaiah. An Historical and Critical Study* (Oxford: Clarendon, 1948), brought up to date by Colin G. Cruse, "The Servant Songs: Interpretive Trends Since C. K. North," *Studia Biblica et Theologica* 8 (1978) 3–27. Many recent exegetes would agree with the view of Claus Westermann: "On principle

"my servant" has prevailed and is now honored. In the thanksgiving psalms "the many" can designate the large group who look upon the vindication of the poor person and hear the story of his rescue. "He put a new song in my mouth, / a song of praise to our God. / Many will see and fear, / they will trust in Yahweh."[13] "With my mouth I will give great thanks to Yahweh; I will praise him in the midst of the many."[14] The kings of the world are included in the many who are astonished at the transition from sub-human disfigurement to exaltation as servant of Yahweh. In Second Isaiah what happens within Israel is often viewed by the "nations/kings." Kings saw the commission of the servant in 49:7 and were stunned. In fact the entire scene in chapter 49, the honoring of the servant and the revival of Zion, is expressly announced to "coastlands and far off peoples" (49:1). The astonishment of the many shows the spontaneity of the divine act. In 48:6c–8, the utter novelty of the new creation was expressed by asserting that no one had heard of it before today. "You have not heard, you have not known, / your ears were not opened hitherto" (48:8). Cyrus as divine instrument was the unheard-of event in chapter 48; here it is the exaltation of the servant.

The long narrative, 53:1–11b, sandwiched between the two divine pronouncements, tells of the sufferings of the servant and their significance.[15] Is the speaker the "many nations / kings" of 52:15ab who see the servant atoning for their sins and bringing them salvation? The question is important since the speaker is the person or

---

their [the servant songs'] exegesis must not be controlled by the question, 'Who is this servant of God?' . . . The questions which should control exegesis are: 'What do the texts make known about what transpires, or is to transpire, between God, the servant, and those to whom his task pertains?' " *Isaiah 40–66* (Old Testament Library: London: SCM, 1969), 93.

13. Ps 40:3.

14. Ps 109:30.

15. Klaus Baltzer has pointed out that there are two standpoints in the verses. One reports the fate of the servant seen from the outside (53:2–3 and 7–9). The other is the viewpoint of a commentator on the sufferings of the servant and their significance for the community (Is 53:4–6 and 10–11b). He goes on to suggest two different speakers. "Zur formgeschichtlichen Bestimmung der Texte vom Gottes-Knecht im Deutero-Jesaja-Buch," in *Probleme biblischer Theologie* (Festschrift von Rad; ed. H. W. Wolff; Munich: Kaiser, 1971) 41.

group whose sin the servant has borne. That the nations are the speaker is unlikely. The nations are mentioned in 52:15ab only because, according to the Deutero-Isaian perspective, what happens to Israel makes visible to them the superiority of Israel's God and the inanity of their own gods. They are part of important scenes as chorus, not as protagonist. The speaker is Israel, more precisely, "the many" who, in the thanksgiving psalms, would have listened to the vindicated just person tell his story, as noted above. By an extraordinary shift in perspective, "the many" tell the story whereas the servant is silent.

The section begins with parallel rhetorical questions in 53:1, the first colon emphasizing the astonishing nature of the report, and the second, the unexpected vindication of one so miserable. In a culture which took destruction and illness as marks of divine disfavor, God's rescue of a destitute or ill person constituted a social rehabilitation of that person. Yahweh's approbation-through-rescue is at the same time a declaration that the poor man's enemies are guilty. The poor person's cries to Yahweh initiate a drama. Will the just God allow evil to triumph or will he vindicate his own nature by rescuing the innocent person? His act is a judgment; the forensic nature of psalms of thanksgiving and of lament is expressed in the frequent metaphor of the law court.

The servant grew like a scraggly plant in arid soil with no beauty to make one notice him. The natural unsuitability of candidates chosen for great mission is often emphasized in the Old Testament. As noted under chapter 49, Moses, Gideon, and Jeremiah all reminded God of their lack of talent. Even David in the estimate of his own family was totally unsuited to be considered as candidate for king (1 Sam 16:1–13). By physical appearance and by sickness the servant seems disqualified for divine commission.

In vv. 4–5 the speakers see that the servant has borne their sins and sickness. Previously they had looked on him, without reference to themselves, as stricken and a target of God's wrath. Now they see that he has borne their sin. That one person can bear the sin of another so as to remove guilt, can suffer vicariously, is not otherwise attested in the Old Testament. In determining the meaning of the concept of this passage one should avoid, on the one hand, reading in

New Testament concepts and, on the other, refusing *a priori* to accept the unique idea as unique.[16]

Our own answer to the difficult question of the meaning of "to bear the sin (or sickness)" of another person is tentative. One must keep in mind that often Hebrew words for sin designated both the act and the guilt (enmity with God) arising from that act. When one commits a sin, the deed itself, independently of the will of the person, generates consequences which have to be borne. During the Exile, this concept of the dynamic act was interpreted to mean that the pre-exilic generation had actually committed the sin but that the exilic generation had to bear the consequences, or the guilt. Lam 5:7 illustrates the idea: "Our fathers sinned and are no more [they are not living so they can bear the guilt], / and we bear their iniquities." Ezek 18:2 is similar: "The fathers have eaten sour grapes, / and the children's teeth are set on edge." The exilic complaint is easy enough to understand. The sinful acts of the prior generations had activated the curses and the exilic generation had to bear the consequences, "bear their iniquities"—concretely exile and the absence of God through the destruction of the Temple.

But how could someone of the same exilic generation like the servant bear the guilt of his contemporaries, "the many"? A partial answer is suggested by the account of the disciples' suffering in 50:4–11, itself drawn from two passages about the disciples of First Isaiah, as was pointed out in the exposition there. The disciples in chapter 50 did not rebel; they offered their back to the smiters, their cheek to those who plucked their beard. We know from the recorded preaching of Jeremiah and Ezekiel that the mass of exiles did not accept their exilic punishment with much awareness of its purpose or with much confidence in their ultimate rescue. Rather most people, buoyed by hopes of a speedy return, talked themselves into thinking that things would soon get back to normal. The enormous inconve-

---

16. H. L. Ginsberg has provocatively stated: "The sense of the entire composition is that the Servant has suffered in order vicariously to expiate the guilt of the many. The idea of vicarious expiation is almost unparalleled . . . hence a natural reluctance . . . to accept the plain meaning of the fourth Servant song. But the scientific method is to accept the unique as unique." *The Book of Isaiah* (Philadelphia: Jewish Publication Society, 1973), p. 21.

nience of the Exile would soon be over. Finally, their hopes dashed once too often, most people decided to settle permanently. Their behavior said that their God was not able to bring them back to his land. But the sin, the guilty state, remained to be expiated.[17] True expiation of the sin would come through conscious awareness of the purpose of the Exile coupled with a lively hope of return. Probably only a minority of the exiles had such sentiments, believers like the author of Lamentations 5 and the disciples of Isaiah. "The many" who endlessly schemed to escape the Exile, first by premature attempts to return and then by decisions to settle in Babylon, can hardly be said to be expiating their sin, to be bearing their iniquities. If the faithless response of the many were the only attitude prevalent in those times, the sin would not have been expiated. But the Exile had come to an end. The many now have to admit that the servant's willing acceptance of guilt made them free of the consequences of their sin—absence from their God in his land.

Vv. 7–9 portray the servant as victimized by an unfair trial. The danger of lying witnesses is mentioned in the Psalms, e.g. 27:12 and 35:11. Whether the servant actually dies as a result of the oppressive trial, as might be suggested by the mention of his grave, is unclear.[18] If he does, then his vindication takes place in heaven and he is given a reward like the servants of Dan 12:3, written almost four hundred years later.[19] Resurrection of this type however is not attested at this period. Resurrection at this time is national revival, like the resurrection of the dry bones in Ezekiel 37. It is much more likely that a "death experience" is described here. The prophet elaborates the experience of "those who go down to the pit," a cliché of lament psalms.[20] The burial of the innocent servant with the wicked, i.e. his being remembered forever as wicked through his grave site, is the

---

17. Sometimes expiation was imagined in quantitative terms, in months or years. Jeremiah's seventy years of punishment is an example.

18. "He was taken away" (luqāḥ) alludes perhaps to Elijah being taken up to heaven in 2 Kgs 2:11, and Enoch in Gen 5:24. V. 8b might well mean what Gen 5:24 adds, "and he was not, for God took him."

19. Cf. H. L. Ginsberg, "The Oldest Interpretation of the Suffering Servant," VT 3 (1953) 400–04.

20. Cf. Pss 28:1; 30:3; 88:4; 143:7; Prov 1:12 etc.

point of the verse. Justice demands that the servant's name be
cleared.

In the last statement of the many, vv. 10–11 (unfortunately obscure through textual damage), the people see the servant rewarded.
His pain and sickness were part of God's plan, not a sign of divine
displeasure. There is a hint in this section, explicit in the next, that
the rescue consists in giving him a share of the land. The phrase "to
lengthen the days" is often used in Deuteronomy, sometimes in con-
junction with offspring, for secure possession of the land.[21] The
phrase "he shall see the light" is one of several important allusions to
Isaiah 8:16–9:7, more than once quarried by Second Isaiah. That
passage describes the darkness of foreign conquest of the land followed by the light of Israelite repossession. It provides Second Isaiah
with a two-stage paradigm for interpreting the Exile. There are at
least two more allusions to it in vv. 10–11. Isa 9:3 speaks of the joy of
repossession as that of warriors dividing the spoil (*bĕhalqām šālāl*);
53:12ab speaks in the same terms, "with the mighty he shall share
the booty (*yĕhalleq šālāl*). The burden that Israel once had to bear
(*subbǎlô*) in Isa 9:4 the servant also had to bear in 53:11d (*yisbōl*).

The declaration of the true state of affairs comes with the divine
speech in 53:11c–12. Yahweh's own plan of righteousness has been
faithfully executed by his loyal servant; the servant is righteous. The
servant's attitude and behavior have made many righteous, accept-
able before Yahweh, by bearing their guilt. They can take possession
of the land and enter Zion where Yahweh's presence can be found.
The reward given to the servant in 12ab, division of the spoils of battle by the victorious commander, is a metaphor from Isa 9:3 and the
surrounding verses. The reward for putting one's life at risk in the
service of the divine commander is the great prize, the holy land.

By a divine decision made public to "the many"—those in Israel
who have not seen and acted with the clarity and obedience of the
servant—the servant's suffering is accepted as valid for the whole
people. The nations look on in astonishment as Israel rises from dis-
grace to salvation.

---

21. For *he'ĕrîk yāmîm* in connection with the land see Deut 4:26, 40; 5:33; 22:7,
and in juxtaposition to *zera'* "progeny," Deut 11:9; 17:20 and 30:18–19.

16th Speech

ZION THE SECURE CITY OF YAHWEH

[54]

¹Shout aloud, O barren one who bore no child,
  lift up your voice, cry out, you who have not been in
    labor.
For more numerous are the children of the forlorn woman
  than of the woman who has a husband, says Yahweh.
²Widen the space for your tents,
  spread the fabric of your pavilions,
  do not hold back!
Stretch out your ropes,
  drive deep your tent pegs!
³To right and left you will expand.
  Your progeny will dispossess the nations,
  the destroyed cities they will inhabit.
⁴Do not fear; you will not be shamed,
  do not blanch; you will not be embarrassed.
You will forget the shame of your youth,
  the humiliation of your widowhood you will remember no
    more.
⁵For the one who marries you is your Creator,
  Yahweh of hosts is his name.
The one who redeems you is the Holy One of Israel,
  God of all the earth is he called.

⁶A wife abandoned,
   broken in spirit,
   Yahweh called you,
the wife of one's youth when she is rejected,
   says your God.
⁷For a brief¹ moment I abandoned you,
   but with great mercy have I taken you back.
⁸In a burst of anger, for a moment,
   I hid my face from you,
but with everlasting devotion I love you,
   says your Redeemer, Yahweh.
⁹It is like the time of Noah.
As I swore then that never again
   would the waters in the time of Noah flood the earth,
I swear (now) that I will never again
   vent my anger against you, rebuke you.
¹⁰Though the mountains totter,
   the hills shift their position,
my love will not totter,
   my covenant of peace will not shift,
   says the one who has mercy on you, Yahweh.

¹¹Afflicted one, storm tossed, unloved,
   here I am to make carbuncles your building stones,
   sapphires your foundation stones.
¹²I will make your towers of rubies,
   your gates of precious stones,
   all your walls of stone.
¹³All your children will be disciples of Yahweh,
   great shall be the prosperity of your children,
¹⁴In righteousness you will be founded.
   Far removed will be oppression;
   you will have no fear.

---

1. The contrast between "brief moment" and "great mercy" is clearer in Hebrew than in English; literally it is "small moment" and "large mercy."

Far removed will be terror;
    it will not come near you.
[15]Can anyone stir up strife without my leave?[2]
    Whoever strives against you will fall.
[16]As I create the smith
    to fan the coals of his forge,
    to make the tools for his work,
I also create the destroyer to ruin.
[17]No weapon fashioned against you can succeed.
Every tongue raised against you in court will be found guilty.
This is the grant of the servants of Yahweh;
    their righteousness comes from me—Oracle of Yahweh.

COMMENTARY

Concern with Zion, interrupted by the speech on the suffering servant in 52:13–53:12, has been constant in the collection since 44:24–45:13, on Cyrus the rebuilder of Zion. Whether indirectly through mention of Babylon in chapters 46 and 47 or directly in 45:14–25, chapters 48, 49, 50:1–51:8 and 51:9–52:12, the focus has not wavered. The final chapters, 54 and 55, likewise center on Zion, the former emphasizing the security of the holy city now that its husband and Creator has returned, and the latter, the city's visibility to the nations as a center of life. The topic in chapter 54, Yahweh rebuilds his bridal city, is not new but the security of the temple-city has not been addressed before with such persistence. The exiles' fear of leaving splendid Babylon for the still ruined and unwalled Jerusalem was deep-rooted enough to require the prophet's attention.

No single proof exists for the unity of chapter 54; a number of points converge to make it probable. There are three sections of approximately equal length, each amplifying points in the previous section: vv. 1–5, 21 cola; vv. 6–10, 20 cola; vv. 11–17, 22 cola. Such balance characterizes other speeches of the prophet.[3] In vv. 1–5 the prophet exhorts Zion to rejoice at her husband's return, which re-

2. The verse is obscure. The translation is a guess.
3. Cf. 40:12–17//18–24//25–31; 41:1–20//41:21–42:9; 48:1–11//12–22; 49:1–13//14–26, etc.

moves the shame of her being without husband and children. Her husband turns out to be her Creator who can accomplish all things. In the next section, vv. 6–10, Yahweh the husband explains that his stay will be permanent. In the last section, vv. 11–17, Yahweh specifies how his presence is to be mediated—through a divinely built temple. The fact that a sacral tent and a temple are to be rebuilt in Zion is no argument against unity. Psalm 84:1–2, 4 describes the Temple both as a "tabernacle" // "court" and a "house" and the examples could be multiplied.[4]

We now examine the three sections in detail. Zion is told to burst into song like the heavens and earth before the creative act of Yahweh which makes her fertile.[5] She is to hymn her God who has taken away her reproach, like the once barren Hannah, the mother of Samuel: "The barren has borne seven, / but she who has many children is forlorn" (1 Sam 2:5). A city is not just buildings but rather the people who live in them. Zion's glory was in her children and her tragedy in their loss and the loss of her husband. Larger tents than before mean that her citizens are now more numerous than in the time of former prosperity.

The old poetry portrayed Zion as "a quiet habitation, an immovable tent, whose stakes will never be plucked up, nor will any of its cords be broken" (Isa 33:20 *RSV*). Ancient Canaanite tradition, even older than the Bible, depicted the god, El, as a venerable patriarch living in a majestic tent complex. The same tradition portrayed other major gods enthroned in their palaces of cedar and stone built upon mountains. The Bible does not always keep the traditions separate. Sometimes it uses both terms to describe the dwelling of Yahweh on Mount Zion, as in the present passage where the first section makes use of tent and the second, a temple. In both sections, the whole city is seen as sacral, a tent- or temple-city. Extension of the sacrality and impregnability of the divine dwelling to the entire city is found elsewhere in the Bible, e.g. in Psalm 48 and Rev 21:9–27. Even Jerusalem's daughter cities, "the cities of Judah" of 40:9, now in ruins, will be filled with Zion's children. The shame attaching to a

---

4. Ps 78:60 speaks of Shiloh as "tabernacle"/"tent" yet the prose tradition in 1 Sam 1:7, 9 speaks of the "house of Yahweh."
5. Cf. 44:23 and 49:13.

woman without husband, children or property—such visible tokens counting for much in biblical culture—will be removed by her husband who is the Creator of the world, v. 5. He can turn the world upside down in favor of his beloved wife.

Like the famous chapter 11 in the eighth century prophet Hosea, the second section, vv. 6–10, locates the taking back of Zion firmly in divine love: " 'Wife of my youth, how could I forget you?' says your God." The promises in the chapter are rooted in Yahweh's word of promise to Israel; the phrase "Yahweh says" or a variant concludes the exhortations in vv. 1d, 6e, 8d, 10e and 17f. Yahweh's brief angry withdrawal contrasts with the duration and magnitude of his love. There is no more danger that Yahweh's fierce anger will again strike Israel than there is that the waters of the flood will again burst upon earth. Love's oath will hold even though mountains and hills are shaken from their place. Even storms paradoxically show the security of Zion, where Yahweh's eternal love is made available to his people.

The last section, vv. 11–17, begins with a reference to those storms of v. 10 which have shaken and humbled Zion. Like the pilgrims to the divinely founded house in the famous prophecy of Isa 2:1–4, visitors to the temple on the mountain receive a teaching (torah) and become disciples. The same thought is expressed in Ps 46:1–3: "God is our refuge and strength, / a very present help in trouble. / Therefore we will not fear though the earth should change, / though the mountains shake in the heart of the sea; / though its waters roar and foam, / though the mountains tremble with its tumult" (*RSV*). In the religious world in which Israel lived, the gods lived in heavenly palaces made by divine craftsmen out of gold, silver, lapis lazuli and other precious materials. Yahweh builds his temple-city, the earthly reflection of the god's house, of precious stones, vv. 11–12. Like the divinely founded house of Yahweh in the famous prophecy of Isa 2:1–4, those who come to the temple on the mountain receive divine teaching, becoming disciples.[6] Prosperity is granted to her children in v. 13b. The righteousness of v. 14, as in 45:14–25, is the order imposed by God upon the world when it was created, the es-

---

6. The same word for "disciples" is used of the servant in 50:4. See the commentary there.

tablished relationships between God and man, man and man, man and nature, and the mutual relationships within the animate and inanimate world. It especially characterizes the city of Yahweh the creator. There can be no injustice in the temple-city, v. 14. The same idea had been expressed in the famous poem Isa 2:1–4: "Nation shall not lift sword against nation, / they shall not learn war any more" (2:4). All is under Yahweh's rule, builder and destroyer both. All are his instruments; thus he can guarantee peace, vv. 15–16. The very last colon, v. 17ef, is to be taken literally. The temple-city is the land grant given to Israel, a renewal of the old land grant of sacral territory under Moses and Joshua. Because Yahweh guarantees his presence in the temple, vv. 9–10, Zion is a secure city.

The whole discourse is a divine speech to Zion telling her that she is to be the site of a now permanent bond of love between Yahweh and his people. They will no longer have to fear the alienation from Yahweh, for it was only momentary and will not recur. To live in Zion is to live in the most secure city in the world.

17th Speech

✓ COME INTO THE LIFEGIVING PRESENCE OF YAHWEH!

[55]

¹Ho, all who are thirsty, come for water,
those who have no money, come!
Buy food for no money,¹
for no payment, wine and milk.
²Why do you spend money for what is not food,

---

1. I emend MT *šibrû we'ĕkōlû / ûlkû šibrû bĕlo' kesep ûblô' mĕḥîr yayin wĕhālāb,* "buy food and eat / and come buy food for no money and for no payment, wine and milk," to *šibrû' ōkel bĕlô' kesep / ûblô' mĕḥîr yayin wĕhālāb,* "buy food for no money / and for no payment, wine and milk." The Old Greek, represented particularly by the uncials A and Q, *badisantes agorasate kai piete aneu arguriou kai timēs oinou kai stear,* "come buy and drink without money and payment wine and fat [*ḥēlēb* for MT *ḥālāb*]," reflects the Vorlage *lkw šbrw w'klw blw' ksp wblw' mhyr yyn whlb.* The Greek translator has characteristically "improved" the awkward *'klw ... yyn,* "eat ... wine," to a smoother *piete ... oinou,* "drink ... wine," on the basis of his memory that Isaiah elsewhere uses "drink" with "wine." The hexaplaric recension reflects MT. At Qumran the ms of 1QIsa^b is missing v. 1, but 1QIsa^a has *šbrw blw' ksp wblw' mhyr yyn whlb.* OG and 1QIsa^a thus agree against MT on a short text—either *šbrw blw' ksp* etc. of 1QIsa^a or *šbrw w'kl blw' ksp* [pointing *'kl* as the noun *'ōkel,* "food," rather than the verb *'ākal,* "to eat," and assuming that the translator missed the idiom *šibrû 'ōkel* and took both words as verbs]. Certainty is impossible since *šā-bar* is hapax in Isaiah and occurs elsewhere, e.g. in the Joseph story either absolutely or with *'ōkel* as object with no difference in meaning. I prefer as original *šibrû 'ōkel bĕlô' kesep* because of the idiom, attested in Deut 2:6 (and 2:28) *'ōkel tišbĕrû mē'ittām bakkesep,* "you shall buy food from them with money"; and, more persuasive still, because of the clear parallelism between vv. 1b and 2a, "Buy food without money ..." and "Why do you spend money for what is not food?" Note too the play on words in *'ōkel bĕlô' kesep,* "food without money," in v. 1a and *kesep bĕlô' leḥem,* "money without bread," in v. 2a.

your earnings for what does not satisfy?
Listen attentively to me and eat choice food,
    enjoy the richest fare.
³Incline your ear and come to me,
    hear and you shall live.
I will make with you (plural) an everlasting covenant,
    the enduring grace to David.²
⁴As I appointed him witness to peoples,
    prince and commander of peoples,
⁵so you (sing.) shall summon nations you knew not,
    nations that did not know you shall run to you,
because of Yahweh your God,
    because of the Holy One of Israel;
    he has imparted his glory to you.

⁶Seek Yahweh where he may be encountered,³
    call upon him where he is present.
⁷Let the wicked man leave aside his way,
    the evil man, his plans.
Let him turn to Yahweh that he may have mercy on him,
    to our God that he may lavish forgiveness on him.
⁸For my plans are not your plans,
    nor your ways my ways—oracle of Yahweh.
⁹For as the heavens are high above the earth,
    so my ways are above your ways,
    my plans above your plans.
¹⁰As the rain comes down,
    the snow, from heaven,⁴
not returning there
    but rather soaking the earth

---

2. The attempts of A. Caquot, "Les 'Graces de David' à propos d'Isaie 55/3b" *Semitica* 15 (1965) 45–69 and W. A. M. Beuken, "Isa. 55, 3–5: The Reinterpretation of David," *Bijdragen* 35 (1974) 49–64 to interpret *ḥasdê dāwid hanne'ĕmānîm* as a subjective genitive, "the reliable manifestations of David's loyalty" (Beuken), have been effectively refuted by H. G. M. Williamson, "'The Sure Mercies of David': Subjective or Objective Genitive?" *Journal of Semitic Studies* 23 (1978) 31–49.

3. Literally, "in his being found." The use of language of visiting a shrine, *dāraš, māḥā'* and *qārôb*, suggests space, not time.

4. The construction of *(ka)'ăšer . . . kēn* is also found in 52:14–15 and 54:9.

making it germinate and bloom,
    providing seed to the sower, bread to the eater;
¹¹So will be the word which goes forth from my mouth,
    not returning to me empty,
but rather accomplishing what I desire,
    succeeding in what I command.

¹²You shall surely go out in joy,
    in peace you shall be led in procession.
The mountains and hills will break forth into shouting before
    you,
    all the trees of the field will clap their hands.
¹³In place of the briar the cypress shall grow,
    in place of the nettle, the myrtle shall grow.
This shall be a memorial for Yahweh,
    an everlasting sign, never effaced.

COMMENTARY

Chapter 55 is an appropriate conclusion to the anthology of speeches. Yahweh's command to his heavenly and earthly servants, "Comfort my people!" in 40:1, empowered Cyrus to dethrone cruel mistress Babylon, leaving the people free to march with the servant to a revivified Zion. The last statement is concrete. It is an appeal to come to the preeminent place where Yahweh may be encountered and where life, i.e. existence with God, may be experienced. If the chapter is broken up into discrete fragments as it generally is by scholars, it loses its realism and becomes instead a quarry for beautiful texts on biblical themes, e.g. on witnessing, on the need to act now, on the fecundity of the divine word.

Unity of composition is made likely by the correspondence of the stanzas: I, vv. 1–5, 18 cola; II, vv. 6–11, 21 cola; III, vv. 12–13, 9 cola. Stanzas I and II are parallel, each inviting people to the sanctuary where life, proximity to the deity, is offered. The last stanza, half the length of the first, concludes the invitation by an announcement of the journey to the shrine. The proportional correspondence between the cola of the three sections, 18, 21 and 9, is like 40:12–31 which is divided into three sections of 18, 22 and 26 cola. The best proof of design, however, is the parallel logic of vv. 1–5 and 6–11; the sections play off one another as they do in 41:1–20//41:21–42:9, 48:1–11//12–22 and 49:1–13//14–26.

We turn to the first section. The invitation to the thirsty and hungry to come and eat freely at the banquet is a genre attested from ca. 1200 B.C. to the second century B.C.[5] When a god or spokesperson for a god uses the formula it is an invitation to a sacred feast at which life is offered. Typically it begins with an offer of food and drink to the hungry and thirsty and ends with an offer of life. The manner in which the offer of life is portrayed can vary but not the essence of the offer: life which consists in proximity to the deity. In a text from Proverbs, Dame Wisdom builds her palace and sends her maids with the invitation: "Whoever is inexperienced, let him turn in here, / whoever lacks understanding, I say 'Come eat of my food, / and drink of the wine I have mixed. / Leave aside folly and live, / walk in the path of insight. / For with me your days will be multiplied, / and the years of your life increased' "[6] The resemblance to the *second* section of the Deutero-Isaian speech is not to be missed: "leave aside" behavior unworthy of Dame Wisdom's dignity and walk in the "way" of wisdom, phrases and ideas found in vv. 7–8. But the affinity with the first section, vv. 1–5, is even more striking— the invitation to eat and drink which is seen to be nearness to the person of Dame Wisdom herself.

There can be little doubt about the meaning of life in Proverbs 1–9. It consists in the intentional search for wisdom, and obedience to it as it presents itself, especially in the experience of the elders. But what is the meaning of the life offered in Isa 55:1–5? It is the covenant made with those invited to the feast. A covenant between God and man establishes a bond between them. In other words, it brings God and man into that proximity which the Bible describes as life. To be in the holy temple-city, to be chosen by Yahweh so that his glory might shine through them to the nations, vv. 3c–5—this constitutes the nearness that gives life to Israel.

---

5. The texts are *CTA* 23.6–7 (*UT* 52); 17.6.2–40 (*UT* 2 Aqht), Proverbs 9 and Sir 24:19–22. I have discussed these texts in detail in "Proverbs IX: A Suggested Ugaritic Parallel," *VT* 25 (1975) 298–306, and in "Isaiah 55: Invitation to a Feast," in the David Noel Freedman festschrift (forthcoming).

6. Prov 9:4–6, 11. Vv. 7–10 are intrusive.

The covenant is the Davidic covenant which installed the king on Zion. "I have set my king on Zion, my holy hill" (Ps 2:4). King and temple were closely associated in antiquity. Second Isaiah no more envisioned the literal restoration of the Davidic monarchy than he did mere revivals of the other institutions from Israel's past. Instead, as we have seen in previous passages on the witness (43:12 and 44:8-9), roles formerly performed by sacred persons like kings and prophets in the past are fulfilled by a wider circle in the new age. It is sometimes said that in Second Isaiah the old royal and prophetic offices are "democratized," i.e. applied to all the people. The term "democratization," if used at all, must be used with discrimination. First, the offices are not simply transferred to the people as a whole but only to those who obey the divine word to return. Second, only one aspect of the whole range of royal duties is transferred here—the king's witnessing his patron God's glory to the nations. As explained under 43:9-44:5, to witness means to demonstrate the god's power to others. Israel is invited to come to the abundance of the banquet. Earthly coinage has no value before the divine splendor. Those who accept enter into the presence of Yahweh, their relationship to him being specified by the eternal covenant which makes the divine glory shine through them.

One more point ought to be made about the first section. In the ancient Near East the building, or rebuilding, of the temple was celebrated with a great feast. The god who built the temple celebrated his kingship represented concretely by the new (or renewed) structure. The previous speech, 54:11-17, narrated the rebuilding of the Temple. Celebration of kingship through a feast is therefore appropriate.

The thought of the second stanza, vv. 6-11, advances like the first: the summons to the sanctuary, v. 6, the insistence upon conduct appropriate to the divine presence, i.e. laying aside profane conduct, v. 7; the movement from food ("providing seed to the sower, bread to the eater") to life as association with Yahweh through commission ("accomplishing what I desire, succeeding in what I command"). V. 6, like v. 1, borrows a formula of call to a sanctuary, "Seek Yahweh!" Such a call underlies Amos 5:4: "Seek me and live; / but do not seek Bethel, / and do not enter Gilgal / or journey to Beersheba." To enter the sanctuary is to enter the divine sphere; behavior appropriate to the profane world is to be left at the door of the sanctuary, as the liturgies of scrutiny preserved in Psalms 15, 24, and Isa 33:14–16 show. The person entering was questioned about the righteousness of his conduct before being admitted. One did not independently walk into the divine presence; one had to be admitted.

Jer 29:10–14 forms an impressive parallel both in expression and in substance to the second section. Vocabulary links with vv. 6–11 are underlined in the following.

> When seventy years are completed for Babylon, I will visit you, and I will fulfill to you my promise, and bring you back to this shrine (*hammāqôm hazzeh*). For I know the plans I have for you, says Yahweh, plans for welfare and not for evil, to give you a future and a hope. Then you will call upon me and come and pray to me, and I will hear you. You will seek me and find me; when you seek me with all your heart. I will be found by you, says Yahweh, and I will restore your fortunes and gather you from all the nations and all the places where I have driven you, says Yahweh, and I will bring you back to the place from which I sent you into exile.

Jeremiah taught that Israel's exilic punishment had to last seventy years after which they would return to "this shrine," in the context an idiom for the sanctuary of Zion. Second Isaiah held the same belief about the divine presence as Jeremiah: Yahweh's glory is definitively revealed only in Jerusalem. Liturgical encounter can take place only in Zion, the place of celebration of the divine victory.

"Many are the plans in the mind of a man, / but it is the purpose of Yahweh that will be established" (Prov 19:21). So runs one of the several proverbs expressing the contrast between the purely human scheming that goes on on earth and the divine planning in heaven that perdures. Such proverbs seem to have influenced the Deutero-Isaian "my plans are above your plans." That all physical life on earth is dependent on heaven should be clear from observing natural phenomena. Water upon which all life depends comes from heaven in the form of rain and snow, fertilizes the earth and provides food, v. 10. The same total dependence of earth upon heaven holds true for the life-giving work Yahweh is now doing—the restoration of Israel in Zion. He has returned to his people; they can now live in his presence in Zion, v. 11.

To come to Zion is to go out of Babylon. Vv. 12–13b echo the call of the first two stanzas by exhorting the people to join a miraculously guided procession through the transformed desert. The highway to home, ringed by evergreens, will remain forever-as a memorial of the great deed of Yahweh. The tree-lined road through the desert will be like the twelve stones that memorialized the crossing of the inhospitable Jordan. The stones were to be "a sign among you; when your children ask you in time to come, 'What do these stones mean?' you shall say to them how the waters of the Jordan were cut off before the Ark of the covenant of Yahweh" (Josh 4:6–7). The defeat of forces hostile to the emergence of Israel as the people of Yahweh must be remembered forever.

In the inaugural vision, 40:1–11, Zion was to announce to the daughter cities what it saw—Yahweh coming back to his holy city at the head of his people. The passage ends with an appeal to all the people of Israel to join that happy procession, making their way across a desert stripped of its power to keep them away from their God and his presence. Will Israel heed the invitation and come to the feast?

INDEX OF BIBLICAL REFERENCES

195

INDEX OF SUBJECTS

INDEX OF AUTHORS